P9-ARU-218

EX LIBRIS

MORRIS DICKSTEIN

08/24
STRAND PRICE
$ 5.00

With the compliments of the author.

Marianne Moore: The Poetry of Engagement

GRACE SCHULMAN

Marianne Moore:
The Poetry of Engagement

UNIVERSITY OF ILLINOIS PRESS

Urbana and Chicago

© 1986 by the Board of Trustees of the University of Illinois
Manufactured in the United States of America
c 5 4 3 2 1

This book is printed on acid-free paper.

Excerpts from *The Complete Poems of Marianne Moore.* Copyright 1935, 1941, 1944, 1949, 1951, 1952, 1953, 1954, © 1956, 1957, 1958, 1959, 1960, 1961, 1962, 1963, 1964, 1965, 1966, 1967, 1968, 1969, 1970 by Marianne Moore. Copyright renewed © 1963 by Marianne Moore and T. S. Eliot. Copyright renewed © 1969, 1972 by Marianne Moore. Copyright renewed 1979, 1980, 1981 by Lawrence E. Brinn and Louise Crane, Executors of the Estate of Marianne Moore. Copyright © 1981 by Clive Driver, Literary Executor of the Estate of Marianne Moore. All rights reserved. Copyright © 1956, 1958 by The Curtis Publishing Company. Reprinted by permission of Viking Penguin Inc.

Library of Congress Cataloging-in-Publication Data

Schulman, Grace.
    Marianne Moore: the poetry of engagement.

    Bibliography: p.
    Includes index.
    1. Moore, Marianne, 1887–1972—Criticism and interpretation.   I. Title.
PS3525.05616Z825   1986   811'.52   85-21006
ISBN 0-252-01270-4 (alk. paper)

*To Jerome Schulman,
for Marcella Waldman,
and in memory of
Bernard Waldman*

Contents

Acknowledgments   ix

Abbreviations   xi

Introduction   1

I. New York: Marianne Moore as
a Characteristic American   9

II. A Way of Seeing: The Poetics of Inquiry   27

III. The Evolution of an Inner Dialectic from
Argumentation to Reverie   43

IV. The Mind's Transforming Power: Metamorphic Imagery
and the Poetry of Engagement   77

V. "A Quite New Rhythm": The Spoken Art of
Marianne Moore's Poetry   97

VI. The Passion for Real Things   117

Notes   123

Bibliography   129

Index   133

Acknowledgments

I wish to thank the editors of the *Quarterly Review of Literature* and *Antaeus,* in which portions of this study first appeared.

I am grateful to the Rosenbach Museum & Library in Philadelphia for permission to use material from their archive. Patricia C. Willis, Curator of Literature, has been especially generous, and her knowledge has been indispensable. I am indebted to Clive E. Driver, literary executor of the estate of Marianne C. Moore, for permission to quote from her published and unpublished poems, letters, and papers, for his painstaking care in reading the manuscript of this book, and for his time and effort in discussing with me matters concerning the work of Marianne Moore.

My thanks go also to Frances Steloff and Andreas Brown for their invaluable help over the years; to Ann Rendall and to her father, E. McKnight Kauffer, for his early guidance; to Ted Weiss and Renée Weiss for their continuous friendship and encouragement; and to M. L. Rosenthal, for his essential aid. Finally, I am more than grateful to my parents, Marcella and Bernard Waldman, for sharing with me their long friendship with Marianne Moore.

Abbreviations

CP	*Collected Poems* (New York: Macmillan, 1951)
CPMM	*The Complete Poems of Marianne Moore* (New York: Macmillan; Viking, 1981)
MMR	*A Marianne Moore Reader* (New York: Viking, 1961)
N	*Nevertheless* (New York: Macmillan, 1944)
O	*Observations* (New York: Dial Press, 1924)
OBD	*O to Be a Dragon* (New York: Viking, 1959)
P	*Predilections* (New York: Viking, 1955)
SP	*Selected Poems* (New York: Macmillan, 1935)
TMTM	*Tell Me, Tell Me: Granite, Steel, and Other Topics* (New York: Viking, 1966)
WY	*What Are Years* (New York: Macmillan, 1941)

Introduction

To read a poem by Marianne Moore is to be aware of exactitude. It is to know that the writer has looked at a subject—a cliff, a sea animal, an ostrich—from all sides, and has examined the person looking at it as well. The practice seems ironic for, by the time of her death in 1972, critics had, by and large, admired, but not explored, a poetry whose own method of appreciation is intensive observation and research.

I hope that this study will contribute a fuller sense of the dimensions of her achievement. I believe that her poetry is concerned with the individual in the modern age, dealing with the impact of essential matters on people who observe, remember and understand. For Marianne Moore looking at an object from all sides also meant talking about it from all sides, and her practice of using rhetorical debates, ranging from simple conversations ("I May, I Might, I Must") to dialectical arguments ("Critics and Connoisseurs") to complex inner arguments ("The Paper Nautilus" and "No Swan So Fine") is actually a method that propels the poems forward and turns our attention to their progress from beginning to end. In fact, the process through which the poems come to terms with the world is fundamental, for their aesthetic elements constitute their form for engagement with larger issues.

The poems of Marianne Moore, with their precise, compact renderings of objects and animals, are concerned with such matters as the courage to endure under brutal pressure; the ordinary virtues of patience and tenacity; the accumulation of diverse impressions that confound the inquiring mind; and the endeavor to maintain personal integrity in a world that encourages fragmentation. This study deals not with those matters but with the poetic methods of presenting them, and for enacting the struggle of the heart and mind to see the realities of this world and to seek "the genuine," or the truths of an ideal realm.

This task seems inevitable at the present time, for Marianne Moore criticism of the last ten years has moved toward a deeper, more serious approach to her work. Before that, fifty years of criticism provided suggestive interpretations that, taken as a whole, present a platform for more intensive evaluation.

From April 1915 through November 1923, when Marianne Moore's writing began to appear in England and America, the dominant question was whether she was a poet. Although magazines such as *Poetry* and the *Little Review* were outlets for the stream of American poetry in which Marianne Moore's work was eventually to flow, editors and critics were still uncertain as to the direction of its currents. Devoted as they were to the new freedom sanctioned by the Imagist movement, believing as they did in Ezra Pound's admonitions to "make it new" and to "compose in the sequence of the musical phrase," editors often disputed the application of those principles. In 1918 Margaret Anderson, editor of the *Little Review*, wrote that she found Marianne Moore's work to be "intellectual" and therefore not poetry, a statement she reprinted in 1953.[1] Although Harriet Monroe, editor of *Poetry*, was among the first to publish her work and was to favor it again in the early thirties, she expressed negative views in 1922. In reviewing *Poems* (1921), Marianne Moore's first book, she objected to what she considered to be arbitrary stanzaic patterns, the absence of growth and climax, and words hyphenated at line endings for pattern rather than for meaning.[2]

The first readers to dissent from those negative critical views were the major poets among Marianne Moore's contemporaries. As early as 1918, three years before the publication of *Poems*, Ezra Pound wrote a letter praising her work and asking for information about her life and poetic methods.[3] In a review of *Poems* that appeared in the *Dial* in 1923, T. S. Eliot wrote, "I can only, at the moment, think of five contemporary poets—English, Irish, American, French and German—whose work excites me as much as, or more than, Miss Moore's."[4] His enthusiasm approached that of Hilda Doolittle (H. D.), who had called her "a perfect craftsman" in an essay published in the *Egoist* in 1916.[5] However, while H. D. had not designated particulars, Eliot cited three elements he found outstanding: "a quite new rhythm," a brilliant use of "the curious jargon produced in America by universal university education," and "an almost primitive simplicity of phrase."[6] In 1925 William Carlos Williams wrote of her work "This is new! The quality is not new, but the freedom is new, the unbridled leap."[7] Writing of her second book, *Observations*, he noted the rhythm, the absence of transitions, unaffected diction, clarity, and the use of anything "so as to illumine it."

From 1925 to 1935, there was a ten-year hiatus in Marianne Moore criticism. While she was editor of the *Dial*, from July 1926 through July 1929, she neither wrote nor published poetry, and eleven years passed between the dates of *Observations* and *Selected Poems*. She recalled taking the work of other writers home with her every night, simultaneously intimating regret for the years of silence and enthusiasm for editorial duties. And despite the rigors of her tasks, the poems that appeared in periodicals from 1932 to 1935 suggest an inner creative activity during her years at the *Dial*.

Since 1935, when *Selected Poems* appeared, Marianne Moore's work has drawn attention and praise from such critics as R. P. Blackmur, Kenneth Burke, John Crowe Ransom and Cleanth Brooks. Although some of their articles, reviews and book-chapters are helpful, others are misleading. Among misguided critical trends is a preoccupation with "syllabic verse," or poetry in which the line lengths of a repeated stanzaic pattern are determined by the numbers of syllables, rather than stresses. The matter of "syllable-counting," which places the typographic appearance of the lines over the spoken rhythmic pattern, has been of interest to many critics since 1935, when it was pointed up by R. P. Blackmur.[8] Even though the poet herself called attention to the syllabic stanzaic pattern in her early work, she later repudiated "syllabics" and "the mathematics of it" as methods of controlling her verse. Although she has undoubtedly used this method at times in her career, visual symmetry being important to her, I believe that the emphasis on "syllabic verse" has distracted readers from the far more important conversational rhythms that are structured on forms of argumentation.

R. P. Blackmur was, though, the first to show the life-apprehending effects resulting from the poet's juxtapositions of the explicit and the strange. This notion of a dichotomy at the basis of her poetry, between imagination and fact, emotion and intellect, ornament and understatement, has been presented in essays by Kenneth Burke, Wallace Stevens and Lloyd Frankenberg. When the imagery of apposition is related to modulations in tone and rhythm, the dichotomy illuminates the poetry's concern with modern attitudes.

The "Marianne Moore Issue" of the *Quarterly Review of Literature* appeared in 1948, adding Wallace Stevens, Elizabeth Bishop, John Crowe Ransom and Louise Bogan to the list of colleagues honoring her poetry.[9] In "About One of Marianne Moore's Poems," Wallace Stevens implies similarities in their ways of discovering the relationship between the word and the thing. In "Marianne Moore," William Carlos Williams contributes a brief but luminous observation: "This is the amazing thing about a good writer, he seems to make the world come toward him to brush against the spines of his shrub. So that in looking at some apparently small object one feels the swirl of great events." Williams's short comment is at the heart of Marianne Moore's achievement: it is not the object itself, however prized—the paper nautilus, the photograph of the fish-shaped bottle—but the depiction of the mind working upon the object, and seeing beyond it to people and events, that is her true concern.

An early instance of the trend toward earnestness in examining her work is the conversion of Randall Jarrell. In 1942 he published a parody of her poetry called "The Country Was," in the *Partisan Review*.[10] Later that year, he wrote an essay proclaiming the need to look more closely at her work and to give her efforts the same attentive reading that she has given others, an admonition that should be established as the golden rule of Marianne Moore criticism. Eleven years later, he wrote an excited appreciation of the *Collected Poems*, but he does not "go through pointing," as he had resolved to do.[11]

Probably Jarrell's most persuasive testament to her range of thought is not in his criticism but in his poems of World War II, which indicate the interaction of their sensibilities. Jarrell's "Eighth Air Force" and "Losses" are so like Marianne Moore's "In Distrust of Merits" and " 'Keeping Their World Large' " in their confessional exploration of conscience as to suggest an understanding deeper than any articulated in his critical prose.

In 1969, three years before the poet's death, Marianne Moore left an archive larger than that of any other major American writer to the Philip H. and A. S. W. Rosenbach Foundation (now called the Rosenbach Museum & Library) in Philadelphia. At the museum are the bulk of her correspondence, her manuscripts and her library, as well as her many notebooks, including reading diaries, conversation notebooks, and poetry workbooks. The *Marianne Moore Newsletter*, published there and edited by Patricia C. Willis, contains letters, documents and checklists, as well as important articles and notes.

The Rosenbach collection marked a new era in Marianne Moore scholarship and criticism. Although three book-length studies had appeared by 1970, the first serious, accurate assessments, informed by material at the Rosenbach archives, are Laurence Stapleton's *Marianne Moore: The Poet's Advance*, and Bonnie Costello's *Marianne Moore: Imaginary Possessions*. Marie Borroff has begun a stylistic analysis, and a number of other critical studies are in preparation.

At this writing, although critics and scholars have the advantage of the Rosenbach archives, readers are hard put to find all of Marianne Moore's published poems and prose pieces. *The Complete Poems of Marianne Moore*, first published in 1967, was reissued in 1981, in a hardcover edition and in paperback. To be sure, there are many revisions, mostly in punctuation (which was of utmost concern to the poet), that were made between 1967 and her death in 1972, and five poems, composed late in her career, were added to replace selections from *The Fables of La Fontaine*. Still, it is not complete.

As for major revisions, they present a difficulty we should be grateful for. They are the lifeblood of the poems, and are fundamental to an understanding of what the body of work consists of. Although the *Complete Poems* is hardly an appropriate title for that incomplete edition, it must be emphasized that the poet fully expected to continue adding to, excluding from, and revising the poems in that edition. And indeed she did, for at least two years after that volume appeared. Nevertheless, many of her most remarkable poems were excluded from that volume and are inaccessible to general readers.

They are, to name just a few: "Dock Rats" and "Radical" (*Observations*, 1924); "Roses Only" (*Selected Poems*, 1935); "Half Deity" (*What Are Years*, 1941); "Melancthon" (*Collected Poems*, 1951); and "Old Tiger," which was never collected (and is included in this study).

Further, the *Complete Poems* and the *Collected Poems* are the only volumes available to the general reader at the present time. The *Selected Poems* and *A Marianne Moore Reader* are out of print, as are her individual books of poems. Patricia C. Willis is completing an edition of Marianne Moore's prose that will supersede her *Predilections*, a book that has been out of print for some time. Actually, then, Marianne Moore's works are available primarily to readers who have access to libraries with extensive poetry collections. And it is especially important to read all of her works for an understanding of her achievement.

Throughout this work, I have quoted poems from the last collected editions in which they appeared, and from magazine versions only when the poems were not included in editions. My hope is that readers will have greater access to the poems themselves by the time this study appears.

Despite obstacles, critical inquiry continues. One of the negative themes that has persisted since the early days of the *Dial* is that her poetry is limited and small, that it lacks emotion. Another deceptive view is that the poetry is restricted to objects and animals, common and exotic, and that it concentrates on the acquisition of details about things, largely at the loss of more universal considerations. This theme, which is affiliated with the belief that the poet, a collector of curios, does not evoke deep feeling, was foreshadowed by Ezra Pound's statement, in 1919, that the poems would not sell widely because they demand "mental attention."[12] Although his prediction, in context, indicts the reader rather than the poetry, many critical evaluations have proved its accuracy.

In the past few years, critics have begun to see its largeness and its passion. My own conviction is that the permanence of Marianne Moore's poetry is in its depiction of a dramatic struggle between the poet's mind and the world. Objects and animals embody the mind's tenacious, life-giving power that

> tears off the veil; tears
> the temptation, the

mist the heart wears,
          from its eyes—if the heart
          has a face; . . .
("The Mind Is an Enchanting Thing," CPMM, 134–35)

In each of the poems, the mind, engaged with an object or animal, moves forward to a fresh, startling idea. In "The Paper Nautilus," the speaker, contemplating the sea animal taking care of her eggs, works through to the idea of love as "the only fortress / strong enough to trust to" (CPMM, 121). The notion is at once parallel and antithetical to the "entrapped writers" and the authorities at the outset of the poem, since we find in each statement about the nautilus a reference to the limited people. In this way the mind, exploring everything about an object, has seen beyond it to the world.

Hers is an art of perception: to feel deeply is to see clearly, to peer beyond surfaces, and to explore permanent truths. The poet amasses facts, remarks, observations, details from guidebooks and manuals, in pursuit of answers to the mysteries of modern love, of heroism, of timeless values we treasure in the face of a world that urges fragmentation. Frequently, though, the assemblage of information only provokes further speculation, as we learn when the speaker of "People's Surroundings" declares, after contemplating sophisticated knowledge in a modern city, "These are questions more than answers" (CPMM, 56).

Her poetry of the mind's inward growth is enlivened by metamorphic imagery that dramatizes the progress of consciousness in its shifts from one vivid scene to another. That view of a fluctuating world is a commonplace among scientists and philosophers of the age, who have doubted the validity of an unchanging reality. "What is more precise than precision? Illusion," asserts the speaker of "Armor's Undermining Modesty" (CPMM, 151), affirming that principle. Common in the poetry, and coinciding with moments of perceptual change, are figures of fire, water, and rock, elements of metamorphosis. Other images are dialectical in that they move and are moved, act and are acted upon, see and are seen. These images, and the ways in which they are manipulated, enact the struggle of consciousness toward illumination.

To be sure, the poetry's form for engagement evolves throughout her career. While retaining the naturalness that is essential to her craft, she develops an inner dialectic, a rhetorical scheme that imitates the mind's growth through change. It proceeds from the early conversation and, later, from the metaphysical dialectic, which involves a combination of direct address and formal discourse, and the use of an extended image to display the argument. Superimposed on this pattern is the image of "seeing" that dominates her later poetry; the figure grows out of the earlier impulse of meditation that requires having to see an object before analytic reasoning can take place. Further, in each phase of her work, rhythmic divisions correspond to shifts in tone within the schemes of argumentation. Her compelling, spoken cadences are the result of this careful patterning.

A proper understanding of her achievement requires patience, attention, and humility. Although inquiries are made and solutions are not easily found, the quest creates the tension between the world and the object on which the mind dwells. For every position there is a refutation; still, the mind gains, for it moves forward by containing its antithetical elements. Just as dignity is attained through hardship and freedom rises above the limitations that life imposes, wisdom results from the dangerous endeavor to perceive.

I

New York:
Marianne Moore as
a Characteristic American

Ezra Pound was the first of Marianne Moore's major contemporaries to see the largeness of her concerns, and to find that her work was rooted in an American tradition imbued with foreign effects. Further, the very form of her poetry of engagement was bolstered and, in fact, inspired, by their friendship.

In 1918 and 1919 Marianne Moore, in New York, and Ezra Pound, in London, exchanged letters that indicate what kind of woman and poet Marianne Moore considered herself to be at the age of thirty-one. Responding excitedly to poems she had submitted for publication in the *Little Review* ("a very good ear" and "your stuff holds my eye"), Ezra Pound inquired about her life, her methods and to what extent she had absorbed American and European influences. In a letter dated 16 December 1918, he wrote:

> How much of your verse *is* European? How much Paris is in it? This is, I think, legitimate curiosity on my part. If I am to be your editor, and as I am still interested in the problem of how much America can do on her own.

Her correspondent was curious about his native country, and about New York:

> Do you see any signs of mental life about you in New York? I still retain curiosities and vestiges of early hopes, though I doubt if I will ever return to America. . . .[1]

Pound also asked specifically about the effects of the French or Greek poets on her work:

> I want to know, relatively, your age, and whether you are working on Greek quantitative measures or on René Ghil or simply by ear (if so a very good ear). . . . I wish I knew how far I am right in my conjecture of French influence; you are nearer to Ghil than to Laforgue. . . . (*Letters*, 142–43)

In answer to his questions about her American background, Marianne Moore gave a concise account of her early years:

> I was born in 1887 and brought up in the home of my grandfather, a clergyman of the Presbyterian church. I am Irish by descent, possibly Scotch also, but purely Celtic, was graduated from Bryn Mawr in 1909 and taught shorthand, typewriting and commercial law at the Government Indian School in Carlisle, Pennsylvania, from 1911 until 1915. In 1916, my mother and I left our home in Carlisle to be with my brother—also a clergyman—in Chatham, New Jersey—but since the war, Chaplain of the battleship Rhode Island and by reason of my brother's entering the navy, my mother and I are living at present in New York, in a small apartment.[2]

Marianne Moore's most vivid description of life in America was of the neighborhood in which she lived, at 14 St. Luke's Place, in Manhattan: "I like New York, the little quiet part of it in which my mother and I live. I like to see the tops of the masts from our door and to go to the wharf and look at the craft on the river." Writing of those wharves in "Dock Rats," which was to appear in *Others* in 1919 and to be abandoned after its publication in *Observations* (1924), the poet who enjoyed observing things in her own locality also glimpsed remote cultures in a ship's cargo that included "a parrakeet from Brazil" and "a monkey . . . all arms and tail; how delightful" (O, 53–54).[3]

To Ezra Pound's questions about influence, Marianne Moore replied that she knew no Greek and had not read extensively in French; she knew neither Ghil nor Laforgue, and did not know of any tangible French influence on her work. She was later to change that view and repeatedly declare her indebtedness to French writers after Ezra Pound brought it to her attention in 1918. At that time, however, she wrote that she was aware of the direct influences of Gordon Craig, Henry James, William Blake, the minor prophets, and Thomas Hardy. Two years later, in an unpublished essay of 1920, entitled "English Literature Since 1914," she was to praise Joseph Conrad, for his "hard-twisted, aristocratic quality," and the "cumulative strength in his emphatic, expertly narrated tales"; W. W. Hudson, for being given over to "precise seeing," and for having "predominently the scientific attitude of mind in conjunction with spiritual vision"; George Bernard Shaw, for being "aristocratic in feeling," and for having "a relish of what is modish and deft"; Max Beerbohm, for "the range and particularity of . . . observation"; and many others.[4] In a letter of 1925 to Caspar Harvey of the Missouri Writer's Guild she wrote of her enthusiasm for certain prose writers, such as Francis Bacon, Defoe, Bunyan, Thomas Browne, Leigh Hunt, and Burke.[5]

Coming to maturity in the first two decades of the century, when many artists were finding new sources of American creativity in foreign cultures, Marianne Moore stayed at home and lacked the wide-ranging experience of her contemporaries. Of the five major figures born in the years 1883 to 1888 (William Carlos Williams, 1883; Ezra Pound, 1885; Hilda Doolittle, 1886; Marianne Moore, 1887; T. S. Eliot, 1888), Pound, Eliot and H. D. were established residents of London by the end of World War I, and Williams had studied abroad. Marianne Moore, on the other hand, visited Europe only once during the early years, in the summer of 1911, with her mother.

Marianne Moore was born in Kirkwood, a suburb of St. Louis, on November 15, 1887, ten months before T. S. Eliot, and near his birthplace. For the first seven years of her life, she and her mother and brother lived with her grandfather, the Reverend John Riddle Warner, pastor of the First Presbyterian Church in Kirkwood. After his death, her mother, an English teacher, took her two children to Carlisle, Pennsylvania, where Marianne attended the Metzger Elementary School and the Metzger Institute, a secondary school for girls. She was to return to Carlisle after her graduation from Bryn Mawr in 1909, when she taught stenography at the United States Indian School for more than three years.

Entering Bryn Mawr in 1905, Marianne Moore majored in economics and history, minoring in biology and spending much of her time in biological laboratories. An article in *Current Biography* states that the poet "was burning with the desire to write but did not feel at ease in academic English."[6] "I felt at ease, but the required stand was eighty," she said, and wrote in the margin, "I did not have the required stand in English!" According to a comment in the *Marianne Moore Newsletter*, "Her desire to pursue 'Major English' as a junior was thwarted by low marks in the course and her professors' reports that in her prose she was obscure and often failed to express her ideas or to make her point."[7] At the same time, there were consolations. In an interview with Donald Hall (1961), she said that her laboratory studies affected her poetry profoundly, especially with regard to "precision" and "economy of statement."[8]

In August 1968 I asked her if she would tell me about the first poets she met who had influenced her work. She replied:

H. D. was my classmate in 1908. In 1910, after my graduation, she invited me to contribute to *The Egoist*. (I didn't, until much later.) She sent me a beautiful picture, though. I looked at it and said, "Is this my classmate?" She wore her hair with bangs and had large clear eyes, in the classical Greek style.

I think T. S. Eliot was the first poet who was strikingly a poet in my eyes. He and Edmund Wilson had an appointment to come to tea at my house in New York one day. I had turned heaven and earth upside down to prepare for their visit.

Then they didn't come! Edmund telephoned that T. S. Eliot had to go to a party, and would I come there instead. My mother said, "Well, I wouldn't think of it. I would answer him politely but I wouldn't stir one step. It's very inconsiderate—if not rude—to make plans weeks in advance and at the last minute to say no."

Well, I went. Gilbert and Mrs. Seldes and I had a splendid time. Thinking of my mother and her propriety, though, I knew I couldn't join them for a *week*. I left early, shortly after T. S. Eliot arrived. I have no pride.

I was tremendously pleased with T. S. Eliot, never having met him and having heard of him for years. It was an *event*. People praised him, and you wanted to see for yourself how it is.

Marianne Moore's description of her first meeting with T. S. Eliot, which took place in 1933, illustrates her characteristic conflict between propriety and the desire to discover things at first-hand. Confronted with a choice between pride and experience, she opted for experience, developing a direct though elegant manner.

The poet's early life, which may seem more secluded than the lives of her contemporaries, was actually an ideal background for her poetry of response to common lives and commonplace things. Although her approach to subject matter changed throughout her career, she chose essentially the same kinds of material, which included elephants she had seen in a lecture-film on Ceylon, an icosasphere she had read about in *The New York Times*, a chameleon whose photograph she had seen in *Life*, a fifteenth-century tapestry reproduced on postcards, an exhibit of sixteenth-century Persian treasures. Her poetry carries forward the American tradition in its use of what is about, and in its insistence on the poet's freedom to contemplate any subject without diminished energy. For her, being an American was, as she wrote of her countryman in "Henry James as a Characteristic American," " 'intrinsically and actively ample, . . . reaching westward, southward, anywhere, everywhere,' with a mind 'incapable of the shut door in any direction' " (P, 31).[9]

That 1934 essay was one she cited in a letter to Dorothea Gray as being descriptive of her "outlook on life."[10] In the essay she marks the writer's passion for ordinary things, his affection for family and country, and his enjoyment of objects to the extent that "no scene, strange accent, no adventure—experienced or vicarious—was irrelevant." She was to stress this love of real things throughout her career; in 1960, she wrote in "Brooklyn from Clinton Hill": "for anyone with a 'passion for actuality' there are times when the camera seems preferable to any other medium; or so I felt in 1896, enthralled by Lyman Howe Travelogues at the Opera House in Carlisle, Pennsylvania. As sequel to lantern-slides, cosmoscope, and stereopticon, Brooklyn Institute movies were Aladdin's Magic" (MMR, 187).[11]

Besides Henry James, Ralph Waldo Emerson was another of the "characteristic Americans" to influence her work, and it was through Emerson, most likely, who also moved Walt Whitman, that Whitman's music found its way into her early work. Although she did not value the Camden poet, their resemblances cannot be ignored. For example, the following passage is from "Dock Rats" (1920), published in *Poems* and *Observations*, but excluded from editions after 1924:

> the square-rigged four-rigged four-master, the liner,
>   the battleship like the two-
> thirds submerged section of an iceberg; the tug
> dipping and pushing, the bell striking as it comes; the
>   steam yacht, lying
> like a new made arrow on the
>
> stream. . . .
>
> (O, 53)

And the second passage is from Whitman's "Crossing Brooklyn Ferry":

> The round masts, the swinging motion of the hulls,
>   the slender serpentine pennants,
> The large and small steamers in motion, the pilots
>   in their pilothouses,
> The white wake left by the passage, the quick
>   tremulous whirl of the wheels. . . .[12]

Both are poets of place, creating wonder in the landscape and things of America, in this case, lower New York Harbor. Both passages are written in an acervate style, the accumulation of detail forcing the reader's attention on the poet's process of thought. True, Whitman's clusters of detail show a growing relationship between poet and scene, while Moore's acervate style emphasizes the scene itself, leading to a joyful concluding statement: "shipping is the / most interesting thing in the world." Nevertheless, the excitement of either passage is in the sense of a mind set in motion by the amassment and reiteration of detail.

It was Emerson, though, who preceded Whitman in his use of lists and related methods. Although Marianne Moore did not mention Emerson early in her career as being one of the writers she most admired, she did refer to him in a 1963 "Voice of America" broadcast, and in her notes to "The Student."[13] Their affinities are subtle, but surely there. In Emerson's poetry and prose, the use of lists to objectify emotion resembles Marianne Moore's use of lists in "The Monkeys," "People's Surroundings," "The Steeple-Jack," and "England." Both share the concern with the process of attaining knowledge through visual perception.[14] Her acervate style, and her important technique of epanilepsis in "The Grave," bear likeness to some of Emerson's poems, as well.

Ezra Pound, on the other hand, was interested in an American culture amalgamated by foreign and historical influences, but one that had been inaugurated by Walt Whitman. Pound recognized only in Europe that he was guided by the spirit of Whitman. He wrote, in *Patria Mia:*

> I believe in the immanence of an American Renaissance . . . Whitman established the national *timbre.* One may not need him at home. It is in the air, this tonic of his. But if one is abroad; if one is ever likely to forget his birthright, to lose faith, being surrounded by disparagers, one can find, in Whitman, the reassurance. Whitman goes bail for the nation.[15]

Although their interests and admirations differed considerably, Marianne Moore and Ezra Pound shared the belief in a poetry of facts, science, and common lives. There is no doubt, also, that her correspondence with Ezra Pound stimulated her enjoyment of commonplace things, as well as the air that was to become unmistakably hers: the insider's skilled knowledge of how things are done, from engines and clocks to baseball and tennis. In a letter dated 10 May 1921, two and a half years after their first exchange, she wrote to Ezra Pound:

> You imply that what we are doing in America might be of interest to the artist in Europe; it is, of course, important to me. . . .
> It would give me pleasure to write to you personally of anything that comes up that you might not know of, that I know would interest you. Such books as Avowals, Heloise and Abelard, the Life of Henry James are important, but immediately on publication they are common property. . . . I have been interested most, in the last two years, in technical books such as

Gilman's Museum, Ideals of Purpose and Method, . . . Harold
Baynes' book on dogs, the Earthenware Collection by G. Wool-
iscraft Rhead, McGraw's and Matthewson's books on baseball
and Tilden's book on tennis.

This last is a little crude as when it says that a tennis racquet
is an introduction to any town, but it is sound and aggressive
both from the point of view of sport and of art.[16]

With an adventurous enthusiasm that is of our native variety, she
wrote to her friend in London of foreign material and of American
events, carefully differentiating between them. In the same letter of
1921, she wrote:

The chief events of interest in town this winter have been
Yvette Guilbert, the circus, the Cabinet of Dr. Caligari, a German moving picture film with a cast and set of great exotic
beauty, and the Beggar's Opera.

As for native material, I think we have it in Wall Street, in Dr.
Williams, and in e. e. cummings as a poet and as a critic. . . .

Although Marianne Moore was to celebrate Ezra Pound's achievement in later essays, the letter of 1919 indicates no indebtedness to
her friend. In fact, when Pound asked whether her metric was
influenced by his early work, she replied politely, though not without jocularity: "The resemblance of my progress to your beginnings
is an accident so far as I can see. I have taken great pleasure in both
your prose and verse, but it is what my mother terms the saucy
parts, which have most fixed my attention" ("A Letter," 17).

However, the part of their correspondence concerning the poems
she had sent to Pound reveals that she made certain revisions on the
basis of his gentle suggestions, and that the effects these changes
served became fundamental to her later work. For example, where
Pound suggested she lower some capital letters, she lowered all—
except after full stops. He had written: "When you break words at
end of line, DO you insist on caps. at beginning of next line? Greeks
didn't, nor does Ghil. Not categorical inhibition, but . . ." (Letters,
143). She replied, "To capitalize the first word of every line, is rather
slavish and I have substituted small letters for capitals in the en-
closed versions of the two poems you have" ("A Letter," 17).

Thereafter, lowercase letters were used for lines beginning with
the latter parts of broken words. Further, after the 1921 edition of

Poems, lowercase letters were used at the beginnings of all lines that did not begin new sentences, and all previous poems were changed accordingly. When this change is considered with a host of revisions the poet made later in her career, such as the alteration of hyphenated words at line breaks to avoid impeding the conversational flow, we find the lowering of capital letters to be a step in the direction of the naturalness and continuity that evolved throughout her work.

One of the poems she had sent to Ezra Pound was "Black Earth" (later retitled "Melancthon"), in which the poet establishes so close an identification with her subject, an elephant, as to speak for it. The elephant calls itself "Black / but beautiful," in lines whose spoken impact creates empathy with an animal that was rare in poetry prior to her own. However, Ezra Pound, confounding empathy with biography, asked whether she was "a jet black Ethiopian Othello-hued" (*Letters,* 143). Marianne Moore replied playfully that her poem was about an elephant named Melancthon, but that she herself had a fair complexion and red hair.

In the same letter Marianne Moore confessed to feeling estranged from the literary scene, and disappointed with her earliest reception. She wrote: "Originally my work was refused by the Atlantic Monthly and other magazines and recently I have not offered it. . . . I grow less and less desirous of being published, produce less and have a strong feeling for letting alone what little I do produce" ("A Letter," 17). If the formative years were trying, she was later to consider solitude a consequence of her inventiveness. In a 1963 "Voice of America" broadcast, the poet said: "The individuality and emotions of the writer should transcend modes. I recall feeling over-solitary occasionally (say in 1912)—in reflecting no 'influences'; not to be able to be called an 'Imagist'—but determined to put the emphasis on what mattered most to me, in a manner natural to me."[17]

One of the poems Ezra Pound commented on was "A Graveyard," published with that title in the *Egoist* in 1921 and collected as "A Grave" in 1924. The London-based poet had written: "Are you quite satisfied with the final cadence and graphic arrangement of same in 'A Graveyard?' The ends of the first two strophes lead into the succeeding strophe, rightly. The ending

'it is
neither with volition nor consciousness'

closes the thing to my ear" (*Letters*, 142). Referring to an earlier stanzaic version of the poem that she had sent to him, Ezra Pound suggested breaking the line at "is," and changing the word order to "consciousness nor volition." She replied that she preferred the original order, but she did make the change, altering the arrangement of lines in the preceding stanzas for symmetry. Although she maintained the original word order for the publication of the poem in *Observations*, she also revised the poem to free verse for that edition, with line endings corresponding to natural breath pauses. In the same year, 1919, she began to revise other poems from stanzaic to freer structures ("When I Buy Pictures," for example, was altered in a similar way for *Observations*), which suggests that her emphasis on the spoken pattern over visual symmetry had new meaning for her at this time.

Another of the poems she sent to Ezra Pound was "Old Tiger," an astonishing piece that has never been collected, and that has been published only in two journals and in a limited edition, *Omaggio a Marianne Moore*, in Milan. Because it is unavailable to general readers, it is worth quoting in full.[18]

OLD TIGER

You are right about it; that wary,
presumptuous young baboon is nothing to you; and the
    chimpanzee?
    An exemplary hind leg hanging like a plummet at the
    end of a

string—the tufts of fur depressed like grass
on which something heavy has been lying—nominal
    ears of black glass—
    what is there to look at? And of the leopard, spotted
    underneath and on

its toes; of the American rattler,
his eyes on a level with the crown of his head and of
    the lesser
    varieties, fish, bats, greyhounds and other animals of
    one thickness,

the same may be said, they are nothing
to you and yet involuntarily you smile; as at the dozing,
  magisterial hauteur of the camel or the facial ex-
    pression

of the parrot; you to whom a no
is never a no, loving to succeed where all others have
    failed, so
  constituted that opposition is pastime and struggle is
    meat, you

see more than I see but even I
see too much; the select many are all but one thing to
    avoid, my
  prodigy and yours—as well as those mentioned above,
    who cannot commit

an act of selfdestruction—the will
apparently having been made part of the constitution
    until
  it has become subsidiary, but observe; in that expo-
    sition

is their passion, concealment, yours, they
are human, you are inhuman and the mysterious look,
    the way
  in which they comport themselves and the conversa-
    tion imported from the

birdhouse, are one version of culture.
You demur? To see, to realize with a prodigious leap
    is your
  version and that should be all there is of it. Possibly
    so, but when one

is duped by that which is pleasant, who
is to tell one that it is too much? Attempt to brush away
    the Foo
  dog and it is forthwith more than a dog, its tail super-
    imposed on its

self in a complacent half spiral—
incidentally so witty. One may rave about the barren wall
    or rave about the painstaking workmanship, the ad-
        mirable subject;

the little dishes, brown, mulberry
or sea green, are half human and waiving the matter of
        artistry,
    anything which can not be reproduced, is "divine."
        It is as with the

book—that commodity inclusive
of the idea, the art object, the exact spot in which to live,
    the favorite item of wearing apparel. You have "read
        Dante's Hell

till you are familiar with it"—till
the whole surface has become so polished as to afford
        no little
    seam or irregularity at which to catch. So here, with
        the wise few;

the shred of superior wisdom
has engaged them for such a length of time as somehow
        to have become
    a fixture, without rags or a superfluous dog's ear by
        which to seize

it and throw it away before it
is worn out. As for you—forming a sudden resolution
        to sit
    still—looking at them with that fixed, abstracted li-
        zardlike expression of

the eye which is characteristic
of all accurate observers, you are there, old fellow, in
        the thick
    of the enlightenment along with the cultured, the pro-
        fusely lettered,

the intentionally hirsute—made
just as ludicrous by self appointedly sublime disgust, inlaid
    with wiry, jet black lines of objection. You, however, forbear when the

mechanism complains—scorning to
push. You know one thing, an inkling of which has not entered their minds; you
    know that it is not necessary to live in order to be alive.

Marianne Moore's revisions of "Old Tiger," based on Ezra Pound's suggestions, involved methods of composition that were to become fundamental to her growth as a poet. In her letter to Pound she said that the first two lines had originally read

> You are right, that swiftmoving sternly
> Intentioned swayback baboon is nothing to
>   you and the chimpanzee?

and that they were changed to read:

> You are right about it; that wary,
> presumptuous young baboon is nothing to
>   you; and the chimpanzee?
>   ("A Letter," 18)

The result of that revision is the naturalness, a quality she was to characterize, in her essay on Henry James, as being typically American. And the urgency of the altered opening reflects a principle she repeated often in conversations, acknowledging Pound (though changing his actual wording): "Ezra Pound said never, NEVER to write any word that you would not actually say in circumstances of urgency," or "Never, under any circumstances, write what you would not say under emotional stress."

The change in the opening lines of "Old Tiger" was initiated by Ezra Pound, who had written:

I am worried by "intentioned." It is "not English;" in French it is *intentionée*, and I have no objection to gallicisms if done with distinction, and obviously and intentionally gallicisms for a *purpose*. But "intentioned" is like a lot of words in bad American journalese, or like the jargon in philosophical textbooks. It is like a needless file surface (to me—and will upset the natives here much more than it does me). You know, possibly, that I don't mind the natives' feelings, *but* I think that when giving offence one should always be *dead* right, not merely defensible. (*Letters*, 142)

Sending the new lines to her correspondent, she quoted the change and said, "I fully agree with you in what you say about the need of being more than defensible when giving offense" ("A Letter," 18).

The statement is basic to the beliefs of both poets: An unpopular view, a negative opinion, an unfamiliar use of language, must be balanced by the "deadrightness" of absolute precision—the exact word, the image that can be trusted, not simply defended.

Marianne Moore came into herself precociously, having the kind of individuality that normally breaks through only after many years. In some of the early poems, however, there are imitative echoes, especially of Eliot. Pound was quick to check that tendency and draw out her originality, as when, at his suggestion, she changed the end of stanza two in "Old Tiger" from

> And the description is finished. Of the jaguar with the
> pneumatic Feet. . . .

in the original version to

> what is there to look at? And of the leopard, spotted
>   underneath and on
> its toes; . . .

The alteration consists essentially of the change from the jaguar to the leopard image. Although both images have a mysterious, spiritually perceived quality reminiscent of French Symbolist poetry, the leopard image of the revised version, while faithful only to an imagined scene, is concrete. Presenting the change to Pound, she

explained, "Leopards are not spotted underneath, but in old il-
luminations they are, and on Indian printed muslins, and I like the
idea that they are" ("A Letter," 18).

The great result of her changes is precision. Stanza twelve had
read:

> The little dish, dirt brown, mulberry
> White, powder blue or oceanic green—is half human
> and any
>   Thing peacock is "divine."
>
> ("A Letter," 19)

This was changed to

> the little dishes, brown, mulberry
> or sea green, are half human and waiving the matter of
>   artistry,
>   anything which can not be reproduced, is "divine."

Pound had written: "And as for 'peacock': is it the best word? It
means peacock-green??? Or peacock-blue or p. b. green? Peacock has
feet and other colours such as brown in its ensemble???" (*Letters*,
142–43).

The changes show the direct influence of Pound's enjoinder to use
only "the best word." And on the whole the revised version of "Old
Tiger," with its exact, explicit descriptions and objects that come
alive for their precision of detail, does so. Its effects are based on
principles set forth by Ezra Pound: the use of the natural object as
the adequate symbol, rather than the mixture of abstract and concrete; the use of native vocabulary; hardness of diction; precise
rendering of the natural object and emotion. To Pound's principles
she brings an accuracy of the spiritually perceived, or imagined,
detail. She was to write of this practice years later in "Feeling and
Precision": "at all events, precision is a thing of the imagination;
and it is a matter of diction, of diction that is virile because gal-
vinized against inertia" (P, 4).[19]

In "Old Tiger" the poet creates a sense of wonder about the
animals that are, ironically, "nothing" to the tiger, and does the
same for the tiger by describing him only indirectly. The form is an

argument, whose wit results from the juxtaposition of assertions in the tone of direct address ("You are right about it," "what is there to look at?") and illustrations in the tone of discourse. An exclamation, "you / see more than I see" is used to emphasize the central image of sight. That image unifies the speaker and the tiger. In his visual acuity the tiger resembles the speaker, who learns by focusing on appearance, and contrasts with other creatures such as the rattler, whose eyes are *seen*.

The poem embodies an argument on the nature of creativity. The "old tiger," personifying the creative process, sees, realizes, smiles, loves opposition and is, in many ways, one with its subjects. It remains itself only by knowing the inner life of the individual being.

The "old tiger," reminiscent of Blake's tiger, is the seeing consciousness, the artist separated from the select many (or wise few) by his ability to make the imaginative leap. The image of seeing, central to the poem's argument, is similar to Blake's imagery of vision in "The Tyger": "In what distant deeps or skies / Burnt the fire of thine eyes?"

The correspondence of Marianne Moore and Ezra Pound points up their zest for apprehending real things and for finding exact words to present them. Moore was to describe Pound's exuberance for "exact definition" (quoting Hugh Kenner) many years later, in 1931. In an essay called "The Cantos," she wrote: "Instruction should be painless, he says, and his precept for writers is an epitome of himself: teach, stir the mind, afford enjoyment (Cicero's *Ut doceat, ut moveat, ut delectet.*)" (P, 76).[20] As for her own enthusiasm for writing, she quoted George Grosz, the caricaturist, as having said, " 'Endless curiosity, observation, and a great amount of joy in the thing.' "[21] The principle, she felt, applied to her own art, and to the work of others.

The poets were to remain friends, although they did not meet until 1939, and conversed directly only a few times after that. Marianne Moore lived in New York City, Ezra Pound in Europe. They corresponded. When Marianne Moore died, in February 1972, Ezra Pound came out of the vast silence of his later life to recite her poem of 1940, "What Are Years,"[22] at a memorial service for her in Italy. "What is our innocence, / what is our guilt?" he began, and continued to the end: "This is mortality, / this is eternity." It was an eloquent tribute to their affection. He himself died nine months later.

From the beginning, his thoughts were essential to her craft. In the evolving style of Marianne Moore, certain characteristics emerged in 1919 that gathered strength throughout her writing career: precision, naturalness, and the ironic use of an "educated" native vocabulary. Although those qualities had characterized her poetry since its beginning, they were strengthened by Ezra Pound's guidance. And her revisions were in the international American tradition that Pound had heralded in the second decade of the century.

II

A Way of Seeing:
The Poetics of Inquiry

As we have seen, precision is indispensable to Marianne Moore's poetry of excited response to ordinary things. At the same time, "What is more precise than precision? Illusion," we learn in "Armor's Undermining Modesty" (1950); the mind that seeks to understand reality is confounded because it is, itself, a source of wonder. The more we learn about a thing, the less we know of its essential truth. "The power of the visible / is the invisible" is said, in "He 'Digesteth Harde Yron'" (1941), of the camel-sparrow, whose speed is its survival (CPMM, 100, 151).

In an essay quoted earlier, "Feeling and Precision," she writes that precision is "both impact and exactitude, as with surgery" (P, 4). And in an essay written in 1965, "Profit is a Dead Weight," she quotes Henry James as saying of "feelings" that "perception is the height of passion" (TMTM, 23).

Perception is essential to Marianne Moore's poetry of engagement, which affirms the endeavor of the veiled heart, the confounded mind, and the eye that cannot easily see beyond conventional surfaces, to come to terms with the truth of existence in the modern world. Under her inquiring gaze are the wonder of modern love, the proliferation of sights and sounds that crowd the senses, the vast, puzzling structure of the urban metropolis, and the unity that each person strives for in a life that urges disruption. Beyond that, she strives to apprehend permanent truths that are seen by the eye of the mind. So in her early work, we find her constructing an aesthetic of inquiry. And in poems of the thirties and forties, there exists a tension between objects of contemplation and human experience that leads to moments of illumination. Her form for creating this balance begins with her development of an aesthetic for apprehending modern existence.

Her poetics is rooted in the native "instinct to amass and reiterate" that she wrote of in her essay on James, the piece she described, in 1935, as representing her "outlook on life." The poet's reading diaries, nineteen of which are inventoried in the Rosenbach library, indicate the range of her interests. In one of the notebooks, a converted address book whose organizing labels of "Name," "Street," "City" and "Telephone" she ignored for her purpose, she made alphabetical indexes to the quotations, anecdotes, jokes and drawings found in the notebooks. A few of the entries listed in one book under *M*, for example, are: "Machiavelli; MacKenzie; K. Mansfield; Marriage; Masefield; Maugham; Mayran; Medieval mind; Men vs. Women; Mercury; Mechanism of language; Michael Angelo; Middleton; Missionaries, arabs, etc.; J. P. Mitchell; Moderate Party (ad); Monkey; Mountaincraft; G. Moore," etc.[1] The items refer to detailed notes from her reading on strange animals, art objects, and scientific experiments, as well as characterizations from novels and plays. And to preserve the details of things she read about, Marianne Moore would draw pictures. In one of the notebooks, she quotes from an article in the *Illustrated London News* of 6 December 1932, about a Malayan lizard (a creature that appears in "The Plumet Basilisk"), and makes an intricate sketch of the lizard skeleton as seen in a photograph in the *News*.[2]

Marianne Moore began the reading diaries in 1907. One of them, beginning in April 1916, contains a clipping from *Vanity Fair* of Baudelaire's prose poem, "Anywhere out of the World," in English translation. In that piece the poet entices his soul to travel to remote, sunlit countries, but the soul wishes only to get "out of the world," to those places that have the likeness of death.

Marianne Moore had read Baudelaire. Although the most explicit reference, in her prose, to the work of the French poet has to do with his influence on T. S. Eliot, her care in stating that influence suggests her own attraction as well. In an essay, "Reticent Candor," she quotes Eliot as having said, "I think that from Baudelaire I learned first, a precedent for the poetical possibilities, never developed by any poet writing in my own language, of the more sordid aspects of the modern metropolis, of the possibility of fusion between the sordidly realistic and the phantasmagoric, the possibility of the juxtaposition of the matter-of-fact and the fantastic . . ." (P, 54).

For Marianne Moore it was a different matter. Baudelaire and Marianne Moore are poets of inquiry whose resemblances, though basic, are not immediately apparent. Baudelaire's desire to examine the very texture of existence often led him "out of the world," as in *Correspondances*, where the experience of gathering sensations from different spheres produces a union of spirit and sense. Man, crossing a forest of symbols, deciphers the hieroglyphics in nature that conceal reality. Or, he transcends the world by moving inward and beyond the "animal" level of existence, as in *Une Charogne*, in which a decaying corpse emits a strange harmony.

Marianne Moore's investigation of things of this world leads her, at times, into chilly places, as in "Novices" (1923), where half-writers "present themselves as a contrast to sea-serpented regions 'unlit by the half-lights of more conscious art.'" At opposite poles from those pretenders, who are the complaisant "masters of all languages," is "'the spontaneous unforced passion of the Hebrew language— / an abyss of verbs full of reverberations and tempestuous energy'" (CPMM, 61).

Because it is headed for dangerous territory, her examination of human feeling is balanced by an equally strong desire to regulate it. In her essay on James she observes that his "respectful humility toward emotion is brave," despite his warmth and openness to experience (P, 22). And in her poem "The Student," which was revised from a stanzaic to a freer version for its appearance in *What Are Years* (1941), we learn that "study is beset with / dangers," and that the scholar of the title is reclusive "not because he / has no feeling but because he has so much" (CPMM, 102).

In "Marriage," the poet's inquiry into sexual passion results in a clash between perception and emotion:

> Below the incandescent stars
> below the incandescent fruit,
> the strange experience of beauty;
> its existence is too much;
> it tears one to pieces
> and each fresh wave of consciousness
> is poison.
>
> (CPMM, 63)

Peering into the mystery of sexual passion and its manifestation in modern life, the poet finds "the strange experience of beauty" to be capable of demolishing the very process of awareness that would contain it. Love is a mystery because it involves "that striking grasp of opposites / opposed each to the other, not to unity" (CPMM, 69). The speaker (quoting F. C. Tilney, the note tells us), in the voice of a twentieth-century Eve, declares " 'Everything to do with love is mystery' " (CPMM, 69). The jocular tone, cheerfully and self-protectively covering the violence that has been perceived, only deepens the wonder of that mystery.

One of Marianne Moore's earliest poems reveals the clash between searching inquiry and its containment:

THOSE VARIOUS SCALPELS,

those
various sounds consistently indistinct, like intermingled
echoes
struck from thin glasses successively at random—
the inflection disguised: your hair, the tails of two
fighting-cocks head to head in stone—
like sculptured scimitars repeating the curve of your
ears in reverse order:
your eyes, flowers of ice and snow

sown by tearing winds on the cordage of disabled ships;
your raised hand,
an ambiguous signature: your cheeks, those rosettes
of blood on the stone floors of French châteaux, . . .
(CPMM, 51)

The figure of a woman adorned in splendor, her luxurious ornaments assaulting the senses, bears a striking likeness to Eliot's description, in *The Waste Land,* of the richly furnished drawing room in which his lonely, nervous woman sits. The elegant woman is surrounded by artifacts that inundate the senses:

In vials of ivory and coloured glass
Unstoppered, lurked her strange synthetic perfumes,

Unguent, powdered, or liquid—troubled, confused
And drowned the sense in odours. . . .

(ll. 86–89)

Marianne Moore's poem (published at Bryn Mawr in the *Lantern* 25 [June 1917], composed c. 1910–13) precedes his by several years. One of the techniques common to both passages is the presentation of details in one long, syntactically dismembered sentence, calling attention to the vivid imagery, as well as to the speaker's thought process.

"Those Various Scalpels" is essentially a love poem, containing a series of epithets that embody a passionate but futile address to a cool beauty. The poet evokes the similes in *The Song of Songs* ("Thine eyes are as doves behind thy veil"—King James Version, 7:4–5), but makes it new by using ironic metaphors that objectify the speaker's passion and playful rebuke. In Moore's poem the device of anaphora (the repetition of words at the beginnings of sentences or sentence members—"your hair," "your eyes," "your raised hand") gives ritual power to the lines.

If her poem embodies an inquiry into sexual passion, it suggests containment as well, for in the speaker's extravagant tributes to the cruel, cold figure, there are suggestions of pain. And the ending is a startling reversal, distancing the emotion that rises from the beginning of the poem: "But why dissect destiny with instruments more highly specialized than components of destiny itself?"

The life-giving energy, straining against containment and precision of words, is felt throughout her work. In "The Mind, Intractable Thing" (1965), the speaker addresses the mind of the title: "You understand terror, know how to deal / with pent-up emotion . . . I don't. O Zeus and O Destiny!" (CPMM, 208). But always, her scrutiny of human feelings is attended by inner strength, equilibrium and that "reverence for mystery" (CPMM, 9) attributed to the central figure of "The Hero" (1932).

In her 1963 radio interview, she related the world's dilemma to human restraint. The interviewer asked if she was concerned, in poetry, with the question of whether the world has changed, and added: "Does your work envision the appearance of a new human nature, for better or for worse?" She replied:

It preoccupies me, not as timely topics but fundamentally and continuously. Every day it is borne in on us that we need rigor,—better governance of the emotions. We behave like the companions of Ulysses who, "thinking that license emancipates one, Were [sic] slaves whom they themselves had bound;" like the rout in The Green Pastures—like the people of Sodom, causing God to repent of having created man and to consider destroying mankind, so that the angel Gabriel says, "Do dat Lawd, and start a new animal."

I think I see the beginning of a common understanding— some sincerity about "Justice for all."[3]

Both animals are alive in the poetry of Marianne Moore. The old, ungoverned animal displays the unpent energy of the human condition:

> the wild ostrich herd
> with hard feet and bird
>   necks rearing back in the
>   dust like a serpent preparing to strike, . . .
>   ("The Jerboa," CPMM, 10)

The "new animal" is the salamander of "His Shield" (1944), in whose behavior is revealed a formula for men and women: "the power of relinquishing / what one would keep; that is freedom" (CPMM, 144). The lesson of passion and restraint, examining and revering mystery, is basic to the poet's mode of discovery.

Marianne Moore's poetry of engagement evolves from the early years, when she developed an aesthetic inquiry into modern life. In later work a tension between the object and larger issues reveals that the poet, in contemplating small things, is actually struggling through to an understanding of contemporary life: the mystery of passion, the unity of the individual, the timeless values we cherish despite the pressures of life. Making use of traditional modes, she created a form for understanding modern attitudes.

Many of the early poems deal with art, but only as a way of using the artist's vision to penetrate beyond surface appearances. As we have seen in "Old Tiger," the speaker identifies with the artist (tiger)—

> you

> see more than I see but even I
> see too much. . . .

And shares with him the vision of a reality more coherent than ordinary perception. In "Melancthon" (1918) the elephant speaker has the power of spiritual perception:

> I see
> and I hear, unlike the
> wandlike body of which one hears so much,
> which was made
> to see and not to see; to hear and not to hear;
>
> that tree-trunk without
> roots, accustomed to shout
> its own thoughts to itself like a shell, . . .
>   (CP, 47)

Her attitude toward sensibility recalls that of the French Symbolist poets, for whom the artist's vision inspires a more penetrating recognition of the way things are. Her seeing elephant, whose hard, thick surface hides a "beautiful element of unreason" figures forth, despite apparent differences, that concept in Rimbaud's famous *Lettres du Voyant: "Le Poète se fait voyant par un long, immense et raisonné dérèglement de tous les sens."*[4] (The Poet makes himself a seer through a long, immense and rational derangement of all the senses.) In Moore's "When I Buy Pictures" (1921) we learn that a work of art "must be 'lit with piercing glances into the life of things'; / it must acknowledge the spiritual forces which have made it" (CPMM, 48).

Her early work resembles Baudelaire's *Correspondances* in the poet's contrast of external and essential reality, and in her way of presenting the arts as translations of reality in nature. Close to Baudelaire's exaltation of the imagination is "the genuine" of her famous "Poetry" (1919). Here she does not characterize poets as "'literalists of / the imagination'" presenting "'imaginary gardens with real toads in them,'" for those phrases are preceded by the line "nor till the poets among us can be" and followed by "shall we have / it." Although there is "a place for the genuine" in poetry, the genuine is as inaccessible as those human mysteries of "Marriage" (CP, 40–41).

In "The Monkeys" (1917) the cat who sardonically chides critics for their Philistine attitudes remarks that they examine art as though it were deeper "than the sea when it proffers flattery in exchange for hemp, / rye, flax, horses, platinum, timber and fur" (CPMM, 40). *Correspondances* ends with an image of perfumes that have the expanse of infinite things: *"Comme l'ambre, le musc, le benjoin et l'encens, / Qui chantent les transports de l'esprit et des sens"*[5] (Like amber, musk, benzoin, and frankincense, / Which sing the ecstasies of the spirit and the senses). In both passages sensory objects are presented in a conundrum that confuses but challenges the artist's perception.

It is unclear just when Marianne Moore began affirming the convictions of the French Symbolists. When Ezra Pound asked in 1918 how much Paris was in her work, she replied that there was none as far as she knew. She was later to change her mind, recognizing the mysterious nature of influence. In 1961 she told Donald Hall: "Ezra Pound said, 'Someone has been reading La Forgue [sic], and French authors.' Well, sad to say, I had not read any of them until fairly recently. Retroactively I see that Francis Jammes' titles and treatment are a good deal like my own. I seem like a plagiarist."[6] And in a conversation with me seven years later she remarked, "You'll be reading some French author, or Wallace Stevens, and you'll be influenced, and for a while you'll have a touch of it in what you write. Yes, and in your emotions."[7]

In all probability she absorbed the Symbolists' approach early in her career from her readings in English translation. She shares many of their attitudes with her major contemporaries, although many of her early poems predate their work of like concerns. Marianne Moore and T. S. Eliot are poets of ordinary things who break through at heightened moments to the extraordinary, and both transmute the problems of modern life by drawing them into aesthetic spheres. Her treatment of the poet's sensibility is close to Pound's *Mauberley* and the periplum of the *Cantos*. Her idealization of art is akin to that of Williams, and to his conviction that "the world / of the imagination most endures."[8] Like her contemporary, Wallace Stevens, she is chiefly concerned with discovering the relationship between the aesthetic imagination and the natural world. In an essay called "A Bold Virtuoso" (1952), she wrote of Stevens's work: "For poverty, poetry substitutes a spiritual happiness in which the intangible is more real than the visible . . ." (P, 43), and the statement could well apply to her own paradoxes in her vision of reality.

Her treatment of language as an ideal resembles that of Williams in *Paterson*. In "The Past Is the Present" (1915, originally untitled), she writes

> "Hebrew poetry is prose
> with a sort of heightened consciousness." Ecstasy affords
> the occasion and expediency determines the form.
>
> (CPMM, 88)

Ecstasy—that Baudelarian rapture of spirit and sense—plus expedient form are presented in "Poetry" as the fusion of "raw material" and "the genuine" which poets of the present strive for. Her precept, again from "Feeling and Precision," is: "When writing with maximum impact, the writer seems under compulsion to set down an unbearable accuracy . . ." (P, 4). "Poetry" has that formula in reverse, for when its objects are presented, precisely detailed, that constitute the "raw material," that is not it at all: "when dragged into prominence by half poets, the result is not poetry" (P, 41). But "the genuine" remains an unattainable ideal.

In the poetry from 1915 through 1921, animals were used to embody social and aesthetic principles, as in the fables of La Fontaine (which she later translated), Aesop (which she had read early in her career), and Phaedrus. Her poetic manner of fusing animal and human vision is directly related to the fabulist tradition.

The fable, a familiar nursery genre, is actually a complex form whose best performances are lost on children. Since actors have animal bodies and human consciousness, the writer of fables uses animals with ready-made associations to instruct men. In contrast to the epic, whose organizing principle is the heroic myth of man, the fable, which is built on the animal myth of man, has been used as a didactic, prosaic form. Because of this, the best fabulists have revitalized the fable metaphor by presenting animals simultaneously as men and women, and by fusing the comic and serious aspects of the form. Examples of this are La Fontaine's fables, Horace's fables (particularly the human conversations in them, such as the one between the town and country mice), and Chaucer's the *Nun's Priest's Tale*.

Fable writers conventionally defend their use of animals as being suitable to serious poetry. In La Fontaine's *Contre ceux qui ont le goût difficile,* the speaker pretends he is recounting the Trojan War in an effort to please critics who crave something grander than "Aesop's lies"; he swears that if he had Calliope's gifts, *"Je les consacrais aux mensonges d'Esope; / Le mensonge et les vers de tout temps sont amis."*[9] And Chaucer, in the *Nun's Priest's Tale,* explains that he is dealing with Chauntecleer's action because he wishes to turn from abstract to living terms. Referring to a moral argument, he exclaims: "I wol not han to do of swich mateer; / my tale is of a cok, as ye may heere" (ll. 430–31).

It is in the fable tradition, then, at the outset of Moore's "Critics and Connoisseurs," that the speaker states a preference for comic animal actions to the stately elegance of "Ming / products," in which, nevertheless, "a great amount of poetry" is to be found (CPMM, 38). In fables, however, the animal's characteristics are subordinate to its actions. In contrast, Marianne Moore ponders the animal's appearance and behavior. If the fabulist poet uses human beings as part of his animal world, he must fuse human reality with animal behavior to avoid distracting the reader. On the other hand, when a person appears in any of Marianne Moore's early animal poems, she emphasizes the human being who observes, examines, remembers, and learns.

In "Critics and Connoisseurs," the swan image is developed in a way that corresponds to the workings of human memory. The animal is described in a tone of reminiscence ("I remember a swan under the willows in Oxford"), first as a beautiful creature, then as a greedy, tenacious bird, and finally, as a reminder of the experts of the title, addressed in lines that recall the climax of "Old Tiger":

> I have seen this swan and
> I have seen you; I have seen ambition without
> understanding in a variety of forms.
>
> (CPMM, 38)

The climax of "Critics and Connoisseurs" is also a moment of perception, but one that is contrasted more sharply with blindness, in its repetition of "I have seen" and the juxtaposition of seeing with "ambition without understanding."

As in the fable, there is a "moral": "ambition without understanding" is futile. An ant in the speaker's memory, like the unenlightened swan, is unable to learn from past experience and carries heavy burdens though it knows the procedure is useless. The "moral," though, is replaced by a recognition presented as the result of a thought process.

The use of swan and ant to embody principles resembles La Fontaine's techniques in his fables of social comedy, in which the animal reality behind the fable points up the animal laws behind society. But however realistically La Fontaine draws his animals, he has them enact roles based on their appearance or on their associations for the reader. In *Les Animaux Malades de la Peste* (Book Seven, I), a satire on justice in Louis XIV's court, the lion is king because of his majestic and predatory manner. And this is a step more complex than King Noble of *Le Roman de Renart;* the fox, for its sly reputation, is the insinuating polished courtier; the wolf, because of a solemn, doglike face, is the late Renaissance figure of the pedant, a learned adviser who demonstrates that the donkey is the cause of the plague.

On the other hand, Marianne Moore's descriptions of swan and ant rely neither on conventional associations nor on human attributes; the function of their realistic depiction—swan as swan, ant as ant—is to characterize the human being who observes them.

As the fabulist poet mocks laws of social organization, Marianne Moore is concerned, in her early poems, with investigating social attitudes. The world of those poems is populated by obdurate critics, half-writers, literary pretenders, pedantic literalists and dense purveyors of art. With impartiality that is the law of the fable structure (La Fontaine reproves divine right as well as natural right, for example), Marianne Moore chides the "select many" as well as the "wise few" in "Old Tiger." In "The Monkeys" (1917), critics are attacked by a regal cat ("that Gilgamesh among / the hairy carnivora") that is itself distinguished humorously and in surgically precise detail (CPMM, 40).

In her poetry the tension between the object of contemplation and the world can be seen if we follow the progression from the tactile, elaborated imagery of the early poems to the emphasis, after 1920, on visual perception. The imagery of the early poems characterized the poet's perception of experience as a series of intense though fragmented impressions. Reminiscent of Baudelaire's dense visual concentration is the presentation, in "Those Various Scalpels" (c. 1910–1913), of overwhelming sensations crowding the poet's consciousness; "To Military Progress" and "To Statecraft Embalmed" (both 1915) portray warfare and justice, respectively, as chaotic and beyond human understanding. From this disorder emerged her aesthetic with its faith in the power of imagination to transcend the human condition. While the "seeing" speakers of the early poems perceive changes inherent in things, the mind of the later poems, enacting its own process of change, sees things whole.

The later work defines the mode of perception required for knowing reality and expressing its beauty. Marianne Moore's approach to perceiving reality is analytic, although she admires other methods as well, as when she writes of Wallace Stevens's insight "that the 'impossible possible' of imagination is so much stronger than reason that the part is equal to the whole" (P, 37). Her own factual inquiry begins in poems of the early work (before 1921) to the later writing (after 1932). In "People's Surroundings" (1922) human beings with ordinary perception are presented as "those cool sirs with the explicit sensory apparatus of common sense, / who know the exact distance between two points as the crow flies" (CPMM, 56). In contrast, the speaker advocates an "X-ray-like inquisitive intensity" that can penetrate surface appearances. However, this kind of scrutiny is limited: The "exterior and fundamental structure" that is revealed when we see into things is presented at the end of the poem as a vision of workmen and royalty alike, all in their proper places, but in the form of a Whitmanesque catalog so densely detailed as to crowd the senses, concealing as it reveals. Like T. S. Eliot's goal of salvation in *The Four Quartets*, her quest for perception through "X-ray-like inquisitive intensity" is unattainable. But for both poets, the attempt becomes a heroic struggle.

This manner of seeing that is displayed in Marianne Moore's transitional poems can be compared with that of *The Waste Land* and *Paterson*. The modern city of "People's Surroundings," a forerunner whose date of publication actually preceded the other two, is a

> vast indestructible necropolis
> of composite Yawman-Erbe separable units;
> the steel, the oak, the glass
>
> (CPMM, 55)

strikingly similar to Eliot's London:

> Unreal city,
> Under the brown fog of a winter dawn,
> A crowd flowed under London Bridge, so many,
> I had not thought death had undone so many
>
> (ll. 60–63)

and to Paterson, whose "automatons"

> because they
> neither know their sources nor the sills of their
> disappointments walk outside their bodies aimlessly
> for the most part,
> locked and forgot in their desires—unroused.[10]

All three poets fuse modern life with an urban setting in which people behave mechanically because of their lack of insight. In Eliot's city only Tiresias perceives; in Marianne Moore's "necropolis" there are but "noncommittal, personal-impersonal expressions of appearance. . . ." In all of the poems multitudinous sensations characterize the fragmentariness of modern existence and its effect on the sensibility.

That experience of modern life as the simultaneous happening of diverse sensations can be found in many of her poems of this period. In "Marriage" (1923) Eve is "able to write simultaneously" in

> three languages—
> English, German, and French—
> and talk in the meantime;
> equally positive in demanding a commotion
> and in stipulating quiet: . . .
>
> (CPMM, 62)

The cumulative references to vision in "Marriage" are painful indications of the failure to see clearly. After the realization that beauty turns consciousness to poison, Adam and Eve fail to perceive the truth about themselves and about one another. Eve "loves herself so much, / she cannot see herself enough," while in Adam a state of mind "perceives what it was not / intended that he should" (CPMM, 68, 64). In Marianne Moore's poems the failure of perception is equated to the failure of language for, conversely, seeing and words are idealized. In "Novices," for example, half-writers, "blind to the right word," are presented in contrast with the sea, which embodies the strength of the Hebrew language.

The later poems all tend toward this mode of perception. The central figure of "The Hero" has a "sense of human dignity / and reverence for mystery," unlike the "sightseeing hobo" who would know everything she can. The hero knows that reality is not immediately accessible:

> He's not out
> seeing a sight but the rock
> crystal thing to see—the startling El Greco
> brimming with inner light— . . .
> (CPMM, 9)

In "The Paper Nautilus" (1940) the poet combines her inquiry into the world with self-examination. The process of seeing is related to love: the sea animal of the title is presented as "the watchful maker" who "guards" her eggs day and night. From the rhetorical questions at the beginning of the poem, the speaker appears to turn away from the "entrapped" writers and mercenaries to the nautilus constructing her shell. However, the actions of the sea animal are presented in images that refer back to the writers and authorities of the opening lines: "her perishable / souvenir of hope," for example, refers back to "authorities whose hopes / are shaped by mercenaries" (CPMM, 121).

This manner of referring back to a previous image, just as the mind connects figures by association, rather than by logic, is one way in which the poet maintains a continuous tension between the nautilus and the contemporary world. The concluding statement ("Love is the only fortress") is the inevitable outcome of that tension, and it applies to public matters as well as to the eggs of the nautilus. The mind, concentrating on the object, "feeling its way as though blind," finds keys that lead to perception.

In the early poetry the animal embodies the condition or principle that the poet tries to understand. In later poems, such as "The Paper Nautilus," the animal embodies the opposite of worldly values, but animal and human actions are fused in the language.

Marianne Moore's aesthetic of inquiry, then, built on an amassment of fact, combines a courageous examination of human feeling with reverence for its mystery. Making individual use of Symbolist, fabulist, and modern methods, she develops a form whose culmination is the tension created between small objects and larger issues. As a result of this tension, the poet envisions—in "The Paper Nautilus," "The Pangolin," and many other poems of the thirties and forties—a new image of man, the "new animal" that the angel Gabriel would have the Lord begin.

III

The Evolution
of an Inner Dialectic
from Argumentation to Reverie

In Marianne Moore's poetry, as we have found, the passion for discovery of real things leads to a tension between the desire to amass factual material and, on the other hand, a "reverence for mystery." To imagine the wonders of existence is to move into greater mysteries. A paradox, to be sure, as is her remark, in "Feeling and Precision," that "feeling at its deepest—as we all have reason to know—tends to be inarticulate" (P, 3).

Her manner of inquiry is prefigured in the early work, when the willful speakers of poems such as "Melancthon," "Old Tiger," and "Critics and Connoisseurs" declare "I see" or "I have seen" in climactic passages, or when the self-conscious "I" of "Is Your Town Nineveh?" (1921) declares, "I, myself have stood . . . looking / at the Statue of Liberty" (O, 17).

The process of seeing, or obtaining knowledge by sight, is realized in virtually all the poems that appear between January 1921 and June 1953. The figure of sight may be provided in the conversational opening of a poem ("you've seen a strawberry," CPMM, 125), or may serve an emergent definition, as of the mind in "The Mind Is an Enchanting Thing" ("it's memory's eye"). Although its use is not overly apparent in many of the poems, it is present in all of them, and is fundamental to their structures and meaning. The ubiquity of the sight imagery suggests that her passion for perception is at least as great as her passion for actuality.

This perceptional process is related to a manner of argumentation that is, I believe, at the center of her poetic method. In fact, her form for engagement with modern existence depends chiefly on the development of an "inner dialectic," a process that captures the shifts and contradictions of the poet's mind as it moves forward from contemplating common objects to an understanding of larger issues.

Although this pattern of spoken thought is found only in poems of the thirties and forties, it is implicit in the structures of her poems from the beginning of her career. The method evolves from the rhetorical conversational style of the early experimental poems (1907 through summer 1915), through the discursive, argumentative structures of the poetry (fall 1915 through 1919) to the experiments in self-correction in poems of the transitional period (1920 through 1925). These techniques culminate in a poetic embodiment of the mind's movement from its lower ranges of reverie through stages of waking and knowing to the extreme limits of judgment.

This mode of inner debate had its origins in the impulse to argue with an idea or with form itself that generated Marianne Moore's earliest poetic efforts. In 1968 the poet told me that she began writing in response to "adverse ideas." To illustrate this tendency, she uttered the opening quotation of "Sun," which was first published as "Sun!" in *Contemporary Verse*, in January 1916:

> No man may him hyde
> From Deth holow-eyed.[1]

Speaking of John Skelton's lines, Marianne Moore said, "I wasn't thinking hard about any situation. I just liked what you said naturally, without distortion," adding that she did *not* like the meaning or the form of those lines. Seven years earlier, in her foreword to *A Marianne Moore Reader* (1961), she had written that her negative response was provoked by cadence as well:

> I dislike the reversed order of words; don't like to be impeded by an unnecessary capital at the beginning of every line; I don't like, here, the meaning, the cadence coming close to being the sole reason for all that follows, the accent on "holow" rather than on "eyed," so firmly placed that the most willful reader cannot misplace it.

In "Sun" she presents a series of images that transform and contradict those of the opening lines, creating a rhythmic pull between the initial idea and the one that follows.

Her mode of argumentation is characterized by marked qualities at definite intervals throughout her career.

Rhetorical Conversations

Nearly all her poems appearing before fall 1915 are rhetorical arguments that fall into three groups: the first includes poems that are addressed to human beings or conventional attitudes, as, for example, "I May, I Might, I Must"; the second comprises poems whose speakers address abstract concepts, such as "To Military Progress"; the third consists of poems addressed to idealized figures, such as "That Harp You Play So Well," in which King David is the silent listener.

An example of the first type of argument is "Progress," the first poem she remembered having composed, in 1907, at Bryn Mawr, and the eighth to be published, appearing in *Tipyn O'Bob* in June 1909.[2] Marianne Moore allowed the poem to remain uncollected for fifty years, then retitled it "I May, I Might, I Must" for its inclusion in *O to Be a Dragon* (1959). It reads in its entirety:

> If you will tell me why the fen
> appears impassable, I then
> will tell you why I think that I
> can get across it if I try.
> (CPMM, 178)

The speaker is a witty conversationalist, for whom the argument is at least as important as the endeavor, as we gather from the repetitions of "why" and "tell me." The adversary is a pedantic person. And the contrast between the "I" and the "you" is emphasized by conditional understatements ("if I try," "I think that I"), phrases that characterize the speaker and also serve the natural effect.

Naturalness is the striking quality of this poem, and it was also Marianne Moore's earliest objective. "Do you think it sounds natural, as in real life? As though I am talking to you? That's what I think it ought," she said to me of her poetry in April 1967, and quoted those lines from "Progress" as an illustration of the conversational ease that had been her goal from the beginning. "I don't want it artificial," she insisted, "and it ought to be continuous. . . . There, everything comes in straight order, just as if I had not thought it before and were talking to you. Unstrained and natural. Well, that's an extreme example, too. I don't do that well. I'd like to. And so, some of my things *do* sound thought up and worked over."[3]

The "natural" element in "Progress" is tone. Less so is the rhythm in octosyllabic couplets whose lack of metric variation creates a sustained, taunting effect. However rigid, though, the rhythm does not hinder the continuity that later devices were to permit to a greater extent. She was to attribute to Ezra Pound her concept of poetry as urgent speech, and yet the conversational urgency is found in the first poem she remembered having composed, its naturalness disciplined by the argumentative tension between the "I" and the "you."

A less successful poem, "To an Intra-Mural Rat," appeared in *Poetry* in May 1915, was placed as the opening poem in *Observations*, and then, wisely, was abandoned. Whatever its flaws, however, it serves as another example of the first type of argument between speaker and adversary. It reads:

> You make me think of many men
> Once met, to be forgot again
> Or merely resurrected
> In a parenthesis of wit
> That found them hastening through it
> Too brisk to be inspected.
>
> (O, 9)

Here the "you" of the rhetorical conversation is the rodent of the title who reminds the speaker of an offensive lot. The element that is antithetical to her emerging style is the way the cadence conduces to the placement of unnatural stress, especially in the fifth line. The basic iambic meter forces the unnatural accents "*hastening* through it," which recall her objections to the nonconversational accents in Skelton's lines. Unnatural stresses seldom are found in her poems, though, even in the early years. And again, the reason for pointing them out is to show that they do not, for the most part, impede the conversational flow.

"To Military Progress" (1915),[4] another of the poems from the early experimental period, is an example of the second kind of rhetorical argument, involving the speaker and a principle or condition addressed allegorically as "you." Although the rhythm is more natural, the vagueness of the central image is antipodal to Marianne Moore's emerging poetics: it is a "warped wit" separated from body, heart and soul, laughing at its fallen torso. The dismembered figure is likened to the concept of armed power, but the poet's usual visual precision and clarity are not found in this early poem.

The third kind of conversation, involving the speaker and an idealized figure, is exemplified by "That Harp You Play So Well" (*Poetry*), in which the "you" is King David; "To a Prize Bird" (originally published in the *Egoist* as "To Bernard Shaw: A Prize Bird"), in which the figure addressed is Shaw; "To William Butler Yeats on Tagore" (the *Egoist*), in which the listener is Yeats; and "The Past Is the Present" (*Others*), addressed to Habakkuk. All were published for the first time in 1915.

Marianne Moore used the "I" and "you" polarization in nearly all of the poems published before 1917, in their original versions if not in the later variants. In some cases the tension between "I" and "you" was relaxed in later versions: for example, the variant of "Sun" ("Fear Is Hope") that appeared in *Observations* is clearly a rhetorical conversation, and the "we" and "you" encounter is presented more dramatically than in later versions. After the early twenties discursive development becomes the exception rather than the rule, and the use of the intimate "you" is less frequent. However, the poet's early work with the rhetorical scheme led to important developments in the later poetry.

Metaphysical Argumentation

The early "metaphysical" style characterizes poems published in periodicals for the first time in fall 1915. The style reaches its culmination in "Old Tiger" and "Critics and Connoisseurs," whose primary satiric and dramatic effects result from subtle shifts in tone in conversations the speakers are holding rhetorically with the figures of the titles. The method involves the combination of direct address and formal discourse, and the use of an extended image as a rhetorical device to display the argument. In his introduction to Marianne Moore's *Selected Poems*, T. S. Eliot described the tone of "The Monkeys" (1917) as "a fusion of the ironic-conversational and high-rhetorical." That fusion is fundamental to the "metaphysical" dialectic in her poems of these years.

By "metaphysical" I mean the "intellectual, argumentative evolution" that Sir Herbert Grierson admired in the poems of Donne, rather than poetry that is "metaphysical" because it is governed by a conceptual system. Remarkably similar to the "strain of passionate, paradoxical reasoning which knits the first line to the last" in poems of Donne and Herbert is the rhetorical scheme of assertion and illustration that provides the dynamics of Marianne Moore's compositions of 1915 through 1917.[5]

Superimposed on this rhetorical pattern is the "meditative" action in seventeenth-century poems. Louis L. Martz has described the importance of the contemplative practice in poems of that period and of its survival in modern poetry, as in the work of Wallace Stevens and D. H. Lawrence. Methodical meditation, he writes,

> satisfied and developed a natural, fundamental tendency of the human mind—a tendency to work from a particular situation, through analysis of that situation, and finally to some sort of resolution of the problems which the situation has presented. Meditation focused and disciplined the powers that a man already possessed, both his innate powers and his acquired modes of logical analysis and rhetorical development.[6]

Marianne Moore had read the seventeenth-century poets at Bryn Mawr,[7] and was raised in a Protestant tradition that had assimilated the work of Richard Baxter, the seventeenth-century American Puritan author of *The Saints' Everlasting Rest*, a book she quoted from, much later, in her poem "Marriage." Its meditative practices bear many resemblances to those of the Jesuits. Apart from direct influence, however, the meditative impulse was in the air that Donne had breathed, as well as in the atmosphere of her contemporaries.

The discipline of meditation, which involves having to see a thing before the process of analytic reasoning can take place, illuminates the image of "seeing" that dominates Marianne Moore's later poetry, as well as her manner of collecting information about things. Early and late we find in her poetry, as we do in the structures of

Donne and Herbert, the unification of a rhetorical pattern by the attempt at close analysis and elaboration of the thing seen.

Another "metaphysical" characteristic that leads to an understanding of her achievement is her method of disparaging a subject to make it more impressive.[8] The tendency is important in considering Marianne Moore's use of diminishing figures, for her seeming dispraise excites wonder and makes subjects noteworthy. Further, she unifies her rhetorical patterns by closely analyzing those subjects she derides. In "Old Tiger," for example, the poet's negative amplifications of animals that are supposedly inferior to the beast of the title actually enlarge their stature. And her lively descriptions of those creatures further the argumentative progress of the poem. The method recalls Donne's "The Sunne Rising," in which the lover's complaints against the sun set the rhetorical pattern in motion, and the extensive elaboration of the sun image binds together the discursive movement of the poem. But where Donne used this technique to create a logical orderly exposition, Marianne Moore, in the modern tradition, employed it to approximate a process of feeling.

"To a Steam Roller," which appeared for the first time in the *Egoist*, 1 October 1915, prefigures the metaphysical style in its pattern of assertion and illustration. The dialectic is not as fully developed as it is, for example, in "Critics and Connoisseurs," in which shifts of tone develop the complexity of the argument and of the person who observes, analyzes, and perceives. In addition, an object is used as an embodiment of the "adverse idea," but only partially so: In places the speaker's remarks could only refer to the crushing machine of the title ("Sparkling chips of rock"—CPMM, 84); in others they refer to the idea of using steamrolling tactics ("You lack half wit"). Nevertheless, the poem represents an important stage in the direction of metaphysical argumentation.

It opens with an ironic understatement: "The illustration / is nothing to you without the application." The speaker is an elegant conversationalist, but in a distinctly American way, indicated by the use of Latinate words in the tone of direct address, the quality of speech that Eliot referred to in his essay on Moore as "the curious jargon produced in America by universal university education—that jargon which makes it impossible for Americans to talk for half an hour without using the terms of psychoanalysis."[9] What is even more curious is that despite fashions in colloquial usage, educated

American jargon has not changed substantially since T. S. Eliot described it in 1923, and that the poet's witty rendering of it has a remarkably contemporary effect.

The poem continues with lines that amplify the opening assertion:

You lack half wit. You crush all the particles down
    into close conformity, and then walk back and forth on them.

The second stanza begins with a precisely detailed description of what the pulverizing machine does: "Sparkling chips of rock / are crushed down to the level of the parent block." At this point the tone shifts again to the discursive conversational level ("Were not 'impersonal judgment in aesthetic / matters a metaphysical impossibility'"), when the speaker is reflecting on what has been vividly seen. In the final statement the leap in tone from "metaphysical impossibility" to "butterflies" heightens the irony of the notion that fragile creatures might attend upon the crushing mechanism, as well as the irony of using the steam roller as the subject of a serious discussion.

What the speaker has told the steam roller is simply that its mechanical, conformist approach is useless in aesthetic matters. The poem derives its humor, though, from the incongruously elegant conversation that the speaker is holding rhetorically with the devastating force. The assertions and analytic reflections are understated ("I can hardly conceive," "but to question"), while the machine's actions are positive ("You crush all the particles down").

The function of the vivid imagery, which begins to appear at this stage of her development, is to advance the argument by displaying the figure. Unlike the "fen" in "I May, I Might, I Must," the steam roller, with its "sparkling chips of rock," is closely seen, and its delineation serves the rhetorical development. Also, the dazzling, though disparaging, amplification betrays the speaker's fascination with the brutish force. The diminished object is watched carefully enough to be of great interest, and this conflict between degradation and curiosity supports the argumentative tensions that enliven the poem. Finally, the rhythm, freer than that of earlier structures, allows unhindered conversation and permits greater concentration on the speaker's complexity of thought.

"Critics and Connoisseurs" (1916)[10] has, in addition to the fable overtones that we saw earlier, a rhetorical pattern that is typical of Marianne Moore's early poems of metaphysical argumentation.[10] Its tentative opening assertion, "There is a great amount of poetry in unconscious / fastidiousness" (CPMM, 38), resembles the openings of Donne's early lyrics (such as "If yet I have not all thy love") in its way of bringing the reader into the middle of a situation, and of capturing the attention without arresting it. The speaker of Marianne Moore's poem is a dignified American conversationalist, as we know from the fusion of formal and informal rhetoric that characterizes the "educated" native jargon ("A great amount of poetry").

The lines that follow amplify the opening assertion. To "Certain Ming / products, imperial floor coverings of coach- / wheel yellow," the speaker prefers spontaneous endeavors such as making "a pup / eat his meat from the plate." The use of such homely assertions recalls the graphic similitudes that bring home the opening assertions in some of the poems of George Herbert ("Lord, how can man preach thy eternall word? / He is a brittle crazie glasse"—"The Windows," ll, 1–2). It is similar to that practice of seventeenth-century poets, based on methods of meditation, of combining rhetoric with a vividly imagined scene. In addition, the leap from "certain Ming / products" to "a pup," and the introduction of small animals into a serious argument provides irony that serves the satire.

The structural function of the irony in the first stanza is to set into motion the dialectic that moves the poem forward. As Rosamund Tuve explains, in *Elizabethan and Metaphysical Imagery*, the first requirement of the dialectic method "is that the contrary of a position, later refuted, must be stated with authoritative power, or, in poetry, with utmost vividness."[11] In Marianne Moore's poem the familiar jocular image of making "a pup / eat its meat from the plate" undercuts the dignity of "Ming / products," thus countering it. Throughout the poem images are presented vividly and then disparaged in a way that contributes to the portrayal of the speaker, as we shall see.

In stanza two the tone shifts to reminiscence:

> I remember a swan under the willows in Oxford,
>   with flamingo-colored, maple-
>   leaflike feet. It reconnoitered like a battle-
>   ship. Disbelief and conscious fastidiousness were

> ingredients in its
>   disinclination to move.

The swan is a beautiful bird, its comeliness musically reinforced by stressed vowels ("re*mem*ber," "swan," "*Ox*ford") and by assonance ("leaflike feet"). In the fourth line of the stanza the tone shifts again ("Disbelief and conscious fastidiousness"): the swan becomes a greedy, stubborn creature that "made away with what I gave it / to eat," and the tone of anger is achieved by the use of clipped vowel sounds ("its," "bits," "disbelief"). What began as a magnifying appraisal ends as a diminishing one, for the swan is transformed in the process of calling it back. The modulation of tone from nostalgic reminiscence to anger, a highly complex but natural-seeming device, shows this writer's masterful observation of human, as well as animal, behavior. In this poem she has presented a memory that changes in the very process of detailed recall, enacting, by changes in imagery and tone, the mind's changing view of reality.

That analysis and understanding of the memory lead to the climax of "Critics and Connoisseurs":

> I have seen this swan and
> I have seen you; I have seen ambition without
> understanding in a variety of forms.

Unenlightened striving, or "ambition without / understanding," is the principal idea to which the poem builds. The language recalls that of seventeenth-century poems whose meditative structures require tactile perception, such as Henry Vaughan's "The Search" ("I have been / As far as Bethlem, and have seen"—ll. 5–6) and "The World" ("I saw Eternity the other night"—ll. 1). Here the address is ironic, for the critics and connoisseurs would be unable to perceive its meaning.

At this point the tone shifts again to reminiscence for an illustration of what has just been understood:

> Happening to stand
>   by an ant-hill, I have
>   seen a fastidious ant carrying a stick north, south,
>   east, west, till it turned on
>   itself, . . .

The speaker's wonder at this useless pattern is emphasized by the sixth repetition of "I have seen," and by the difficulty of observing, from a standing position, the detailed activity of the ant.

The concluding question refers back to swan, ant, critics, and connoisseurs:

> What is
> there in being able
> to say that one has dominated the
> stream in an attitude of self-defense;
> in proving that one has had the experience
> of carrying a stick?

In "To a Steam Roller" the object is only a limited embodiment of crushing by devastating force: at times the speaker addresses a machine ("you crush all the particles down") and at other times, an abstract idea ("you lack half wit"). But the swan and ant of the later poem embody the condition of being those dense pretenders of the title. The effect is more natural in that the animals are never addressed directly; instead, the poet presents the creatures in imagery whose language refers back to critics and connoisseurs. The swan's "proclivity to more fully appraise bits" is at once a description of the bird and a polite reprimand to the critics. "Dominated the / stream" and "carrying a stick" refer to swan and ant, respectively, and also to critics and connoisseurs. Although the technique is intricate, the effect is unstrained. Because of the conversational tone and the speaker's politeness, such reproaches might be implied but are never stated outright. At that, the double meanings would be understood only by the more intelligent listeners, not by the persons addressed as "you."

The poet has presented a subtle dialectic on the nature of perception ("I have seen") as opposed to blind action ("ambition without understanding"). In the first stanza an idea is presented and illustrated, although we do not know until the concluding question that the poet's true theme is the absence of perception, and not "unconscious / fastidiousness." In the second stanza the idea is altered by means of a shift in tone from discursive argument to recall, and the change is mimetic of a memory that is transformed from a magnifying appraisal to a diminishing one. In the third stanza the poet clarifies the implications of the idea and, in the conclusion, illustrates the readjusted theme. The argumentative evolution is supported by the modulation of "fastidiousness" from "unconscious / fastidiousness," describing the "Ming / products" and meaning elegant, to "conscious fastidiousness."

The poet's perception, paradoxically about blindness, is conveyed with astonishing naturalness, especially when one considers the risks of diatribe inherent in such an accusation. The naturalness is achieved through the pattern of assertion and illustration. The poet resembles Marvell, Donne, Herbert, and Vaughan in her way of dramatizing a state of feeling by presenting it and analyzing it in the form of an argument. But while the earlier poet would display an ordered arrangement of thoughts, Marianne Moore presents a complex human being in the process of interpreting feeling. In her poem the accuracy of the image serves the authority of the position that is systematically refuted, in the manner of the dialectic. The swan and the ant are presented in vivid detail before they, as ideas, are refuted. They are diminished, too, not by any system of logic but by an individual in the act of inquiry. A further difference is that while the earlier poets make comparisons between matter and spirit that may be startlingly farfetched, Marianne Moore's imagery is precisely right, provided it is considered as knitting together those leaps in tone that characterize the speaker's recall. It is, however, the method of metaphysical argumentation that is, to a greater or lesser extent, the structure of typical poems that appeared in 1916 through 1919: "Old Tiger," which did not appear, but was composed before 1919; "Black Earth" ("Melancthon"); "My Apish Cousins" ("The Monkeys"); "Roses Only"; "Poetry"; and, perhaps most characteristic, "Critics and Connoisseurs."

Transitional Signs of Inner Debate

The poetry's form for engagement with modern existence can be found by examining its evolution from a "metaphysical dialectic," a pattern of argumentation in which the rhetoric ranges from direct address to formal discourse, to an "inner dialectic," a rhetorical scheme that approximates the mind in its growth by change.

Marianne Moore's poems that were published after 1921 lose the figure of the artist examining the texture of life and art, arguing discursively with some contemporary condition or type. The poet addresses neither abstract concepts directly (as in "To Military Progress," April 1915) nor their embodiment (as in "To Statecraft Embalmed" [1915], "To a Steam Roller" [1915], the early version of "Sun" [1916], "Critics and Connoisseurs" [1916], and "Poetry" [1919]).

The poetry of inquiry into current life gives way to a poetry of psychic change, whose form corresponds to the mind searching out factual knowledge. The perceptional process is related to Ezra Pound's mode of metamorphosis in the *Cantos* and James Joyce's pattern of change, particularly in the "Proteus" Chapter of *Ulysses*, in which objects are presented in such a way as to realize a process of awareness. Unlike the later work of Pound and Joyce, Marianne Moore does not use a mythical system. Nor does her poetry veer toward the spiritual, as T. S. Eliot's later work does. Her materials are in the world of the immediate present, but the approach changes to show the mind exploring the nature of a fluid reality.

As I have said, the seeing speakers of the early poems are replaced by a direct reference to the process of looking, or to obtaining knowledge by sight, which is realized in virtually all of the poems appearing between January 1921 and June 1953. And in the later poetry, visualization is enacted by the devices of inner argumentation.

Those methods of argument evolved throughout the work. Early poems had negative sentence structures reminiscent of Renaissance and "metaphysical" argumentation, such as the opening assertion in "To a Steam Roller" ("The illustration / is nothing to you without the application") and in "Poetry" (1919):

> the same thing may be said for all of us, that we
>   do not admire what
>   we cannot understand: . . .

(CP, 41)

The early negative statements have a persuasive effect not unlike those of Shakespeare ("Not marble, nor the gilded monuments / of princes shall outlive this powerful rhyme"—Sonnet 55, ll. 1–2), and Donne ("Love's not so pure, and abstract, as they use / to say"—"Love's Growth," ll. 10–11).

Related to her use of negative assertions is her modern variant of "correction," defined in *Wilson's Arte of Rhetorique*, 1560, as a method of amplifying a matter by comparing it with one that is greater or smaller. Wilson exemplifies with a statement by Cicero: "We have brought before you my Lords . . . not a theefe, but an extortioner and violent robber. . . ."[12] The device, which was used in many Renaissance and seventeenth-century poems, is found in Marianne Moore's early poems, and conveys the accuracy of the speaker's appraisal: when various animals are described as being "nothing to you" in "Old Tiger," the device of correction amplifies an apparent superiority that is contradicted in the course of the argument.

Evolving from the negative and antithetical assertions that served the discursive argumentation of early poems is the device of "self-correction" that supports the inner argumentative structures of later poems, and corresponds to the imagery of perceptual change.[13]

Self-corrective assertions, expressed in the negative and fused with visual imagery, are among the earliest elements in the mode of inner debate. They can be found in several poems that appeared in 1923 and 1924. The speaker of "Silence" (1924) quotes her father as saying, " 'The deepest feeling always shows itself in silence; / not in silence, but restraint' " (CPMM, 91). That self-corrective statement prepares for the concluding insight, stated in the negative: "Nor was he insincere in saying, 'Make my house your inn.' / Inns are not residences." The father's remarks are about "superior people" who, in Marianne Moore's poetry, are heroes who see more than ordinary people because they revere mysteries that cannot be apprehended. In this poem she stresses the values of perception by defining "superior people" as those who never "have to be shown Longfellow's grave / or the glass flowers at Harvard."

The subject of "An Octopus" (1924), a mountain that is partially hidden from conventional vision, is

> damned for its sacrosanct remoteness—
> like Henry James "damned by the public for decorum";
> not decorum, but restraint;
> it is the love of doing hard things
> that rebuffed and wore them out—a public out of
>   sympathy with neatness.
>   (CPMM, 75–76)

The self-corrective statement, "not decorum, but restraint," leads here to that quality central to creativity, "the love of doing hard things." In her philosophy, set forth in "Poetry" and reiterated throughout her work, the artist may never attain ideal perception, or "the genuine," but it is all in the trying.

In "Marriage" (1923) Adam is unnerved by a nightingale "with its silence—not its silence but its silences." This self-corrective statement precedes a passage in which Adam, blinded by passion, confounds illusion with what is real. And in "To an Egyptian Pulled Glass Bottle in the Shape of a Fish" (1924), the same device ("not brittle but intense") bridges the shift from a distant to a closer view of the glass bottle. In each case the self-corrective phrase, linked with perception, embodies the process of psychic change.

Contradiction, another element in the poetry of inner argument, is an organizing principle of the three pieces that were first published in *Poetry* in June 1932 under the collective title, "Part of a Novel, Part of a Poem, Part of a Play." Although they were not published subsequently under that title, and they appear in *The Complete Poems* separately as "The Steeple-Jack," "The Student" and "The Hero," they do form a three-part sequence and are unified in subject matter and tone. The three figures are listed in "The Steeple-Jack" as being "at home" in the New England town; they are heroic in their manner of seeing reality, each in his own way. In the three poems there are rhetorical shifts from certainty to hesitation, and self-contradictory attempts to define reality.

In "The Steeple-Jack" the shifts in tone are based on contradictory perceptions, rather than on the principles of formal argumentation that generated the shifts of the early poems. It begins with a description of an orderly landscape:

> Dürer would have seen a reason for living
>   in a town like this, with eight stranded whales
> to look at; with the sweet sea air coming into your house
> on a fine day. . . .
>
>   (CPMM, 5)

The scene is described in a deceptively matter-of-fact, chatty tone, and the speaker's enthusiasm for it is controlled, in stanzas one through three, by an intensely detailed presentation of gulls and sea. Both tone and scene change in stanza four as to render the description of order an elaborate disguise:

The

whirlwind fife-and-drum of the storm bends the salt
    marsh grass, disturbs stars in the sky and the
star on the steeple; . . .

Suddenly the scene is presented in imagery of natural violence and, following the change to disorder, the tone shifts again: "it is a privilege to see so / much confusion," the speaker declares, curiously undaunted by the spontaneous disarray. Although both settings are given in the present tense, neither the scene nor the speaker's location has changed. The opening description was of a fair day; this is of a stormy night, and the turn has been too abrupt for a depiction of natural forces.

The process has its roots in devotional exercises that inspired many of the seventeenth-century meditative poems, for example, in one of the spiritual procedures set forth by the English Jesuit Richard Gibbons:

We must see the places where the thinges we meditate on were wrought, by imagining our selves to be really present at those places; which we must endeavor to represent so lively, as though we saw them indeed, with our corporall eyes; which to performe well, it will help us much to behould before-hand some Image wherein that mistery is well represented, and to have read or heard what good Authors write of those places. . . .[14]

This stage of meditation, "composition of place," leads to an analysis of some situation evoked by memory. The mode of meditation here is similar to the one advocated by Richard Baxter in *The Saints' Everlasting Rest*, a seventeenth-century American Puritan treatise— which Moore had read—that focused on joining mind and heart in the act of attentive contemplation. Its manner of concentration can be found in the works of many modern writers, such as D. H.

Lawrence's "act of pure attention." In "Crude Foyer" Wallace Stevens writes

> we use
> Only the eye as faculty, that the mind
> Is the eye, and that this landscape of the mind
> Is the landscape only of the eye.[15]

And in Marianne Moore's later work there are abundant instances of seeing inwardly. In "Granite and Steel" (1966) the bridge is a

> romantic passageway
> first seen by the eye of the mind,
> then by the eye.
>> (CPMM, 205)

According to Marianne Moore's response to a reader, Barbara Kurz, the setting of "The Steeple-Jack" is "both Brooklyn and various New England seacoast towns I had visited." The whales had been found in Brooklyn Bay, she said.[16] The town is meditative, and it lends itself to the poet's creation of a form that will dramatize thought.

The mind's growth by contradiction, figured forth in the sudden change from an orderly to a chaotic landscape, is reinforced by images of "seeing." The words "seen," "see," and "look" are used repeatedly in the first four stanzas, from the opening lines onward, and they are emphasized by assonance. The assonance reaches its highest pitch in the third stanza:

> a sea the purple of the peacock's neck is
>> paled to a greenish azure as Dürer changed
> the pine green of the Tyrol to peacock blue and guinea
> gray. You can see a twenty-five-
>> pound lobster; . . .

Gradually we become aware that the poet is using "sea" as a pun on "see." Its use enables her to reinforce musically the importance of "seeing" and the meaning of perception without resorting to didacticism, and it serves the same function as the perceptive speaker in the earlier poems. The pun incarnates the process of "seeing" false appearances: the detailed description of "seeing" the "sea" is an enactment of the mind's tendency to impose order on chaotic experience. The speaker of this poem imposes the familiar in a situation where the unknown is hazardous. The mind's pattern of growth by punning, a commonplace in the thought process, is found in many of her later poems that present a state of mind, and the ingenious pun on "see / sea" occurs frequently.

In stanza five of "The Steeple-Jack" there is a rhetorical shift from the assertion of the "confusion" to a scene of "the tropics at first hand: the trumpet-vine, / fox-glove, giant snap-dragon, a salpiglossis . . ." and what follows is a list of vegetation whose effect is to control passion. In presenting the luxuriant atmosphere of what purports to be a New England town, the poet holds fear in check by objectifying it, and serves this control by providing a remarkable catalog of exotic plants.

The list fills nearly three stanzas that were deleted from the *Collected Poems* in 1951 and restored in 1961, when it appeared in *A Marianne Moore Reader*. After the list, we hear the elegant, assured conversational tone of the opening lines: a student named Ambrose

> sees boats
>
> at sea progress white and rigid as if in
>   a groove.
>   (CPMM, 6)

From this point on, direct references to "see" and "sea" disappear. But in stanza ten, where the tone veers from certainty, we hear an additional pun on "seeing": The steeple-jack "might be part of a novel, but on the sidewalk a / sign says C. J. Poole, Steeple Jack."

Although the hero, student and steeple-jack rest comfortably in this town, the steeple-jack is really the hero of the poem. True, Marianne Moore knew of a real C. J. Poole who had been hired to repair the steeple of the Lafayette Street Presbyterian Church in Brooklyn.[17] But his name was found treasure, for it is made for the perceptual contrasts contained in the pun: C. (see) J. Poole (sea). In addition, his actions, which dominate the latter part of the poem and succeed references to sight and water, are the heroic ones of placing "danger signs by the church" while "gilding the solid- / pointed star," which, we learn, stands for hope.

The heroism of his task is implicit in the description of the town's chaotic state:

> This would be a fit haven for
> waifs, children, animals, prisoners,
>   and presidents who have repaid
> sin-driven
>
> senators by not thinking about them.
>
> (CPMM, 7)

Here the imagery sharply contradicts the Dürer vision of the opening lines, life's disorders overwhelming the notion of a placid landscape. And the conclusion, with its tone of casual certainty, is contradictory of itself: "It could not be dangerous to be living / in a town like this, of simple people," the speaker asserts, but we know that it *is* dangerous, and that the people are hardly simple. The poet has affirmed either side of the paradox. But the conclusion contains, if not resolves, the opposing positions: the steeple-star "stands for hope." The people have the ability to live with confusion, distrusting perception and yet continually questioning what is real. The steeple-star is no more than a sign of the genuine aesthetic vision, whose attainment is illusory, but there is joy in trying to create it, for this is "the love of doing hard things." The steeple-star is a visible, man-made manifestation of the mysterious quality of hope.

That hope is developed in the second section of the sequence, "The Hero," as patience that is required to live with mysteries we cannot fathom. The hero is one who does not like "deviating headstones / and uncertainty." He dislikes "standing and listening where something / is hiding" (CPMM, 8). But he does. In contrast to "the fearless sightseeing hobo" who must see, or be shown, everything possible, the hero is presented as a "decorous, frock-coated Negro" with a "sense of human dignity / and reverence for mystery" (CPMM, 9).

The second section of the sequence ends with a statement that refers back to the steeple-jack, describes the "frock-coated Negro," and looks ahead toward the student. The hero, we learn, is

         not out
    seeing a sight but the rock
    crystal thing to see—the startling El Greco
      brimming with inner light—that
    covets nothing that it has let go. This then you may know
    as the hero.

The concluding insight, resolving the contradictory perceptions,
is the luminous result of the inner struggle that has been enacted in
"The Steeple-Jack" and "The Hero."

The Inner Dialectic

Marianne Moore's attitude toward change is one I link with a visit
to her home in August 1968. We talked about her poem that had
appeared recently in the *New Yorker*. It begins:

MERCIFULLY

    I am hard to disgust,
    but a pretentious poet can do it;
    a person without a taproot; and
    impercipience can do it; did it.

She spoke about the image of the "taproot" in a way that seemed
fundamental to her poetics of growth by perceptual change. She
said:

A taproot is the center of a plant that is firm in the ground. I
don't like a person with no idea, with mercurial comings and
goings, one who says, "Are you going to a concert? Oh, I think
I'll go, too." That person is always shaping his actions to what
someone else is doing.

I think it's good to have a taproot instead of wavering around.
I think it's good to be positive. But I can't be. I never think that
anything I say is unalterable. I'm always changing things, revising poems. I aspire to have a taproot, but I don't have one. I
don't like dissatisfied people who don't know what they think. I
want to be different, but I am one of those people.[18]

Far from being self-diminishing, she was, in this statement, describing an ideal virtue that she believed no one had the right to claim. "I think it's good to be positive" represented such an aspiration; it was also a subtle tap at the arrogant. In "A Burning Desire to be Explicit," an essay collected in *Tell Me, Tell Me,* she writes of a "positive" woman who questioned the image of "metaphysical new-mown hay" in the title poem of that book. When the poet painstakingly explained in detail the meaning of the compressed image, the woman rejoined, "Well, why don't you *say* so?" (TMTM, 5) Seemingly self-disparaging, her statement actually illuminates her stance toward change. She, as a human being struggling to find what is true, wavered in her understanding. And in the poems, discoveries come out of the struggles of consciousness.

The "inner dialectic," her form for engagement with modern life, develops from the speculative techniques of the twenties to the inwardly argumentative manner of the forties. The method is based on a series of rhetorical shifts that approximate the activity of the mind, focused on an object as its "frame" for examining reality, moving through contradictory perceptions to new ways of examining contemporary ideas.

"No Swan So Fine" (1932) is propelled forward by a process in which the mind attains precision through a struggle with contrasted ideas. The poem opens in the rhetoric of thought, as indicated by the sentence fragment: "No water so still as the / dead fountains of Versailles" (CPMM, 19). The quotation is from an article by Percy Phillip called "Versailles Reborn: A Moonlight Drama," in the *New York Times Magazine,* 10 May 1931. Percy Phillip had observed that despite restoration, the palace and its grounds appeared inert. He asserted, "There is no water so still as the dead fountains of Versailles." Marianne Moore applied the sentence to the photograph, and actually wrote it above the picture in her copy of the magazine.

Like many of her earlier poems, "No Swan So Fine" opens with a negative assertion. However, unlike the earlier poems, whose abrupt, declarative openings had a discursive function ("The illustration / is nothing to you without the application"), the sentence abridgement here denotes reflection. The speaker is mulling over the idea.

At this point, the tone shifts to reminiscence:

> No swan,
> with swart blind look askance

and gondoliering legs, so fine
  as the chintz china one with fawn-
brown eyes and toothed gold
collar on to show whose bird it was.

To convey inward reflection, the poet provides no conversational transition, as she did in the earlier poems ("I remember a swan under the willows in Oxford"). A live swan is juxtaposed with one of "chintz china," and the comic leaps resemble the irony of the earlier poems: the swan's "swart blind look askance / and gondoliering legs" points to the absurdity of the living swan in contrast to the ornamental one; the purpose of the china swan's collar ("to show whose bird it was") mocks its lordly ownership. But while the leaps in earlier poems had satiric effects ("Ming" to "pup" in "Critics and Connoisseurs"), the leaps here imitate associative shifts in the thought process.

According to an entry in the poet's notebook, the swan had decorated a Louis XV candelabra owned by Lord Balfour and sold at Christie's in 1930, after his death. His passing saddened her, as she wrote to George Saintsbury. She was dejected, too, by the passing of the Court of the Kings Louis and, as she wrote to her brother in 1932, by the impending cessation of *Poetry*, the magazine that had displayed American poetry since 1912.[19]

From the opening quotation in "No Swan So Fine," the poet maintains a tension between the world (the lifeless fountains of Versailles) and the object (the china swan). Versailles, once a seat of power and glory, a place where crucial treaties were signed, is quiescent. The tone is elegiac: the commanding, engaging, lively rulers who inhabited Versailles are gone, and in their place the artifact, the crafted object, remains to recall their presence, as well as their transience as mortal beings. In terms of structure, not logic but the flow of thought leads the poet to connect the still waters of Versailles with the china swan, and the associative link is the parallel sentence construction.

In the second stanza the poet concentrates on the ornamental swan:

Lodged in the Louis Fifteenth
  candelabrum-tree of cockscomb-
tinted buttons, dahlias,

sea urchins, and everlastings,
   it perches on the branching foam
of polished sculptured
flowers—at ease and tall. The king is dead.

The poet's excitement for the ornament is objectified by means of
a list that conveys its sensuous luxuriance and that recalls the
exuberance of the past. The clipped final statement ("The king is
dead") is at once a contradiction and an inevitable conclusion. It
refers literally to the death of Louis XV and figuratively, in the
poem's context, to the death of kings. On this level the china swan
links the opening, based on the article in the *Times Magazine* ("No
water so still") and the poet's conclusion ("The king is dead").

However, the final statement might equally evoke a cry of "Long
live the king!" The poet's mind contains the life of the ornamental
swan as well as the death it symbolizes, and her excited description
betrays that fascination. Those characteristics of contradiction and
paradox show the dialectical progress of the mind. The word "everlastings," for example, is a dialectical image in its own right: its
name means forever alive; it is an elegantly sculptured representation of a living flower with a dried, dead-seeming appearance. "The
king is dead" refers back to the first lines, "No water so still as the /
dead fountains of Versailles," and is the mind's way of going back to
a thought that has stimulated the process of recall. It also brings
back the word "fine" in the title, which has the denotative meaning
of "elegant," but carries with it the ambiguous obsolete meaning of
"dead, or deadly" and "immortal."

Although the poet's true impact, here, is elegaic, displaying an ornament that calls back thoughts of its owner, she makes original use
of the elegaic tradition by presenting the mind's process of becoming aware. The china swan is the object on which the poet focuses
thought, operating in a dialectic rather than in a route to a definite
conclusion. Hence, the poet's engagement with the world, marked
by the decline of Versailles, has led to the true subject of "No Swan
So Fine," which is the mortality of living beings and the permanence of art. This realization, however, is given in the form of a
dialectical process of thought that struggles through to the issue by
keeping in view, even as it wanders from, the glimpse of Versailles
in 1931.

The "inner dialectic," then, is the poet's method of presenting

thought in such a way as to see worldly realities. It is not the idea
that is ever at the center of the poetry, for neither poetry nor thought
itself can come to terms with realities in direct, explicit ways. In
any of Marianne Moore's poems whose form is the "inner dialectic,"
the pattern of thought becomes the whole point.

In "The Paper Nautilus" (1940) the contemporary scene is given
at the outset:

> For authorities whose hopes
> are shaped by mercenaries?
> Writers entrapped by
> teatime fame and by
> commuters' comforts?
> (CPMM, 121)

Again, the poet opens with sentence fragments, indicating reverie,
dependent for their meaning on the lines that follow:

> Not for these
> the paper nautilus
> constructs her thin glass shell.

Despite the shift from worldly figures to sea animal, the poet
maintains a tension between them by presenting their differences
and similarities. They are antithetical because of the leap in tone,
and parallel because the construction of the shell is like shaped
hopes and fame's entrapments, all three being enclosures. The suc-
cession of images captures the mind's movement from idea to object
in a pattern of associative leaps.

In the second stanza the poet strengthens this tension between
the world and the object:

> Giving her perishable
> souvenir of hope, a dull
> white outside and smooth-
> edged inner surface
> glossy as the sea, the watchful
> maker of it guards it
> day and night; she scarcely

>   eats until the eggs are hatched . . .
> and then
>   as Hercules, bitten
>
>   by a crab loyal to the hydra,
>   was hindered to succeed,
>   the intensively
>   watched eggs coming from
>   the shell free it when they are freed— . . .

The mutual freedom of eggs and shell calls back the shoddy enclosures of the authorities in the opening lines, and it intensifies the
relationship between the nautilus and her eggs by recalling the
interactions of authorities and mercenaries. Further, the image of
sight is repeated ("watched eggs") and heightened by the pun on
"see" ("succeed"), intimating the blindness of the worldly figures.
    The beautiful concluding lines describe the shell

>   round which the arms had
>   wound themselves as if they knew love
>   is the only fortress
>   strong enough to trust to.
>   (CPMM, 122)

Here it appears that love is not a trap, but a process of reciprocal pro-
tection and freedom. The primary effect of the poem, however, is the
way it moves forward by referring back to previous words ("hopes"
and "eats" for example), just as the mind moves on by referring back
to previous thoughts. The words "fortress" and "trust" recall "the
watchful / maker" of the shell that "guards it day and night." The
poem is concerned with a particular mind struggling to come to terms
with one of the basic issues of contemporary life: the conflict between self-interest and the interest of others. Because its medium
assimilates thought, its references to specific events is oblique: the
reader might, however, be reminded of certain problems of 1940, such
as the Maginot Line, the system of fortifications along the eastern
frontier in France, which gave false security to its builders because it
was supposedly indestructible. The decision of the United States to
participate in World War II can, in fact, be considered in terms of the

central action of the poem: the effects of mutual freedom and the meaning of love as "the only fortress / strong enough to trust to." The central idea is, of course, more general—that of unselfish love—but it is presented in such a way as to show the mind working through to its meaning.

In confessing that she lacked a "taproot," then, Marianne Moore did not mean that she changed convictions mercurially but that she pivoted from one view to another in an honest attempt to come to terms with the complexity of human relationships. The best illustration I know is in the pattern of the poet's conversations. For example, in the spring of 1967 she expressed certain views on war in Vietnam that I thought contradictory, and she spoke for some time before clarifying the logic of her seemingly illogical argumentative progression. She said:

> I try to comfort myself with the thought that they are learning better why they are fighting. But when they say, "This may go on till summer," we are doomed, I feel. I don't dare face it, actually.

Suddenly, the poet veered from our conversation about war and discussed incidents that were apparently unrelated: her ambivalence about a visitor; her divided feelings about an unethical businessman. Then she closed in on her attitude toward war, quoting the last stanza of "The Paper Nautilus":

> round which the arms had
> wound themselves as if they knew love
> is the only fortress
> strong enough to trust to.

> Now that is as specific as I can put it. If you felt that way about any people, you couldn't fight them. You couldn't want to kill anyone. If you permit yourself to be unjust, and sanction it (the golden rule, the same thing) you would not do to others what you would have others do to you.

The poet had used seemingly irrelevant topics as a route to her perception about fighting others simply because they were in the mind's range—as opposed to the staggering notion of unjustified violence. In like manner, Marianne Moore concentrates on commonplace objects and familiar ideas in the poetry, which embodies the mind's route to attitudes about larger ideas. In the poems, though, the center of her attention is the route itself, rather than the conclusive solution.

Just as the wisdom in the poet's conversation seemed to be in its progression from firsthand experience to human destruction, the poetry's greatest aesthetic effects are to be found, I believe, in its assimilation of the massive dialectic arguments of consciousness. The poet comes to terms with ideas not by dealing directly with them, but by creating a form that imitates the mind's devices for struggling through to illumination.

Writing about the mind, Paul Valéry and Sigmund Freud provide insights that are useful in examining the structures of her later poems of the mind. She had, incidentally, read and admired the work of Valéry, while she once remarked that she had not read enough of Freud's writing to gauge his influence upon her. Paul Valéry speculates, in *The Art of Poetry*, that the poet's function is to create in his reader a state of "inner modification" in which sound and sense are unified, and to transform into art fragments of psychic experience fused with present sensation. In his "Introduction to the Method of Leonardo da Vinci" Valéry asserts that the creative process is a struggle with alternative ideas and contradictory images. He writes:

> At a point in this awareness of double mental life which reduces ordinary thought to something like the illusions of a waking sleeper, it seems that the sequence of these illustrations, the cloud of combinations, of contrasts, of perceptions, which group themselves about some study or which float on indeterminately, at pleasure, develop with a regularity that is perceptible. . . .[20]

In *The Interpretation of Dreams* Freud writes that contradiction is a technique of the unconscious:

> Thoughts which are mutually contradictory make no attempt to do away with each other, but persist side by side. They often

combine to form condensations, just as though there were no contradiction between them, or arrive at compromises such as our conscious thoughts would never tolerate but such as are quite often admitted in our actions.[21]

Furthermore, Freud has demonstrated that irony, contradiction, representation through inversion, transformation and similar techniques of apposition characterize the unconscious. He writes:

The way in which dreams treat the category of contraries and contradictions is very striking. It is simply disregarded. "No" seems not to exist so far as dreams are concerned. They show a particular preference for combining contraries into a unity or for representing them as one and the same thing. Dreams feel themselves at liberty, moreover, to represent any element by its wishful contrary; so there is no way of deciding at first glance whether any element that admits of a contrary is present in the dream-thoughts as a positive or as a negative.[22]

I have quoted these passages at length because they illuminate the interior dramas enacted in many of the later poems, gaining striking aesthetic effects from contrasts, contradictions and contrary assertions that lead to sudden insights.

Marianne Moore's war poems evolve as others do, from formal argumentation to inner debate. Among them are "To Military Progress" (1915), addressed to the concept of armed force; "Reinforcements" (1918), built on a polarity between "we" and "they"; "In Distrust of Merits" (1943) and "'Keeping Their World Large'" (1944), both having the form of inner argumentation.

Although "In Distrust of Merits" is a war poem, its central meaning and poetic effects are to be found in the way it captures the struggle of consciousness. It has an interior drama that captures those principles Valéry and Freud ascribed to consciousness. The poem opens with a meiotic rhetorical question: "Strengthened to live, strengthened to die for / medals and positioned victories?" (CPMM, 136). The rhetoric rescues from banality the simple thought about meaningless sacrifice. Like the openings of "No Swan So Fine" and "The Paper Nautilus," the sentence fragmentation indicates neither conversation nor discourse but reverie, involving for writer and reader the whole of the sensibility. Further, the ironic understatement and the repetition (of "strengthened") emphasize the importance of formulating the question, although the idea itself confounds the mind.

Lines three through six contain a subtle contradiction:

> They're fighting, fighting, fighting the blind
>   man who thinks he sees—
> who cannot see that the enslaver is
> enslaved; the hater, harmed.

The dyings are not merely for honors, but for the sake of defeating an enemy blind to the results of its enslavement. Tentatively, the poet perceives there is justification for violence; the insight is gained through paradox ("the enslaver is / enslaved; the hater, harmed"), a device that characterizes poetic speech and also imitates the mental process of moving forward by containing opposites.

The first stanza continues in a tone of prayer, addressed to a "firm star" and to a "tumultuous ocean." The "wave" that "makes us who look, know / depth" is an image of the visual haze that the poet seeks to penetrate throughout. Unlike the enemy, who is blind to the contradictory effects of his behavior, the poet moves through a series of paradoxes to attain clarity. The dialectic between "blind man" and poet is reinforced by puns. "Lost at sea before they fought!" is an outcry whose meaning is vision thwarted by "the mountainous / wave," the pun on "see" referring back to the enemy "who cannot see." The pun imitates the mind as associative, rather than logical, connector.

In this poem, as in " 'Keeping Their World Large,' " the speaking sensibility is a construct of roles for the self. Developing from the dramatic situation of the speaker who declares "I see" and the obdurate adversary of the early poems, the "I" and the "we" of "In Distrust of Merits" are projections of the self struggling for enlightened reconciliation. Just as the rhetorical shifts of "Critics and Connoisseurs," for example, are reinforced by carefully elaborated imagery (as when the speaker's memory of a swan changes in the process of recall), the inward leaps of this poem are supported by imagery of perceptual change.

In stanza one the poet joins others in the prayer to a "firm star,"

and the "we" form is used ("us who look"). The poet then associates
the star with the "stars" that symbolize Judaism and Christianity
("David" and "Bethlehem"), and prays for union of all men ("be
joined at last, be / joined").

In stanza three the poet locates the outer struggle within herself:

> they're fighting that I
> may yet recover from the disease, My
> Self; some have it lightly; some will die. "Man's
>   wolf to man" and we devour
>   ourselves. The enemy could not
>   have made a greater breach in our
>   defenses.

The leap from "I" to "we" is reinforced by the brevity of the three
phrases and two sentences here, which contrasts sharply with the
lengthy sentences of the first two stanzas. The struggle leads to a
new perception: Where the battle had previously been with the
enemy, the "blind / man who thinks he sees," it is now with the
self, which the enemy could not have so disrupted.

The image of the sightless man "who thinks he sees— / who
cannot see" is modulated, in stanza four, to the image of "a blind
man who / can see." The poet perceives that one can evade "a blind
man," but not, as Job knew, one who thinks he knows but does not.

An appeal to the affections leads to the vow, stated in the public
"we" form, never to hate "black, white, red, yellow, Jew, / Gentile,
Untouchable" (CPMM, 137). The poet's inquiry into public moral-
ity concerns the racial and religious brutality that had become, by
World War II, an acknowledged threat to civilization. The vow
recalls the speaker's realization in "The Labours of Hercules" (1922)

> that one keeps on knowing
> "that the Negro is not brutal,
> that the Jew is not greedy,
> that the Oriental is not immoral,
> that the German is not a Hun."
>   (CPMM, 53)

But the differences between them is revealing: The speaker of
"The Labours of Hercules" argues that these are fixed values; in the

later composition, the poet questions only one's ability to cope with these vows.

This inner struggle is conveyed by the "rhetoric" of consciousness, with its coexistence of conflicting resolutions. Throughout, there are contradictions within each of the "we" and "I" figures ("we devour ourselves"; "I cannot / look and yet I must"). In the passage containing the vow, the role of "we"—the poet in concert with others—is emphasized by the placement of "we" conspicuously at the beginnings of two statements of resolution: "We / vow . . . 'We'll / never hate black, white, red, yellow, Jew.'" But a contradictory assertion follows immediately: "We are / not competent" to do so. Next, an interplay between "they" and "we" shifts to a contrast between the "we-they" form and the "I": "They" fight "some we love whom we know, / some we love but know not" and their fighting "cures me; or am I what / I can't believe in?" The sudden turn to "I" suggests that the individual is alone, like Job, rejecting reasons for war that he feels comforted by but knows to be false.

In stanza six the poet appears to reach a definite stance. " 'When a man is prey to anger / he is moved by outside things' "; on the other hand, holding one's ground in " 'patience patience / patience,' " is, paradoxically, " 'action or beauty.' " This statement, whose sententious tone makes it seem a resolution, is actually presented as another of the contradictions of consciousness.

Thematically, it resembles the conclusion of "Reinforcements" (1918), one of her World War I poems:

> The pulse of intention does not move so that one
>   can see it, and moral machinery is not labelled, but
> the future of time is determined by the power of volition.
>   (O, 42)

The invisible "pulse of intention" is, like courageous "patience," an aspect of "the genuine" that is ideal but unattainable. But in the later poem destruction and stalwart inaction are displayed as part of the dialectic that structures the composition. "Fighting fighting fighting" and "patience patience / patience" are set against one another in phrases that are thrown into relief by falling rhythm and lack of punctuation, a technique that emphasizes the process of perceiving the nature of an idea by contemplating its opposite.

Moreover, the repetitions of words characterize the speaker as one who is painfully trying to understand. We are hearing the speech of the mind, which moves forward by containing antithetical elements.

Using imagery and language reminiscent of the Book of Job, the poet cries out in the role of the solitary self, "I cannot / look and yet I must." Although the outburst recalls the climactic statement of "Critics and Connoisseurs" ("I have seen" blind striving), the rhetoric has gone inward; referring back to "the blind / man who thinks he sees," its self-correction indicates the resolution to see by means of the transforming process of the mind. Then, if the fighting "can teach us how to live, these / dyings were not wasted" is another apparent resolution that is actually a struggle between contrasts, suggested by the juxtaposition of "live" and "dyings." These contradictions lead to the insight of the final stanza, where the poet pivots from the "we" to the "I" and locates the cause of war deeply within the "hate-hardened heart" (CPMM, 138).

At this point the poet presents the principal theme toward which the poem has been building:

> There never was a war that was
>   not inward; I must
> fight till I have conquered in myself what
> causes war, but I would not believe it.
>   I inwardly did nothing.

The passage conveys a resolution, but it is one that is arrived at through containment of contradictory assertions, much like Job's resolution through tragic understanding. "There never was a war that was / not inward" is a negative assertion mimetic of the mind's tendency to represent through the opposite. That war lives inward is, though, in the context of this poem, a definite assertion. The "I" resolves to fight hate "in myself"—but at the same time cannot believe in the self. And the changes in tone that accompany the "I" figure throughout are parallel to the modulation in tone of exclamatory "O" cries from the rhetoric of public prayer ("O shining O / firm star") to censure, still in the "we" form ("O alive who are dead, who are / proud not to see") to personal contemplation ("O . . . I cannot / look and yet I must," "O heart of iron") to the personal passionate outcry ("O Iscariot-like crime!").

The struggle for illumination resembles Job's tragic quest for insight, and there are structural similarities to the Book of Job. While the biblical work is built on a dialogue of voices, its protagonist moving toward understanding through self-analysis, Marianne Moore's poem embodies a dialogue of the mind between the "I" and the "we," and moves toward resolution. The ending is an open one, comparable to the "dance to the measure" at the end of Williams's *Paterson*. In "In Distrust of Merits" the poet asserts belief in the aesthetic imagination ("Beauty is everlasting"), but not in the reconstruction of the fragmented self, the "dust" that continues to walk the earth.

In 1952 Marianne Moore quoted an important lesson from Confucius, which she found in Ezra Pound's *The Great Digest and Unwobbling Pivot*. The quotation reads: "If there be a knife of resentment in the heart or enduring rancor, the mind will not attain precision" (P, 82). That statement is a gloss on the relationship between the heart and mind as it is presented in "In Distrust of Merits," an interaction of personal integrity, for it involves a response of the whole of the sensibility.

"In Distrust of Merits" is structured on a process of purifying the heart through intensive self-analysis, and of joining heart and mind in the act of attentive contemplation. The practice is one that D. H. Lawrence, Hopkins, Yeats, Stevens, and many other modern writers have resuscitated from the seventeenth-century meditative tradition.[23] It is structured also on the "inner dialectic," true to the mind's way of moving forward. The questions raised in the poem, about the individual's ability to cope with love, are essentially unanswered. Although the poet finds illumination in the creative act, she does not envision the removal of psychic resistance that would put an end to human destruction. But neither is there an end to inner war, for the rhetorical tensions of the poem are unresolved. The interplay of the "I" and the "we," the modulated imagery of sight, progress to the end in a tense coexistence of conflicting opposites. There is no "moral" to the dialectic in this poem concerning inner war and outward battle, since the progression of consciousness permits no final reconciliation of conflicting attitudes.

IV

The Mind's Transforming Power: Metamorphic Imagery and the Poetry of Engagement

In the poetry of Marianne Moore three kinds of images enact the struggle of consciousness toward illumination. They are: metamorphic images, such as fire, water and rock; contrasting images, such as the live swan and the china swan in "No Swan So Fine"; and images that are dialectical in that they move and are moved, act and are acted upon, see and are seen ("enchanting"/"enchanted," "enslaver"/"enslaved").

The endeavor to achieve awareness is fundamental to her work. In the Rosenbach Museum & Library there is a copy of Paul Valéry's *Monsieur Teste* (New York: Knopf, 1947) with Marianne Moore's extensive handwritten notes inside the front and back covers. There she scrawled her thoughts about "his preoccupation with consciousness." She wrote: "The mind—and the drama of consciousness is the subject of all Valéry's work," and "Valéry saw in Leonardo da Vinci the whole mind, that generalized awareness which includes, comprehends all we know." Of these notes Patricia C. Willis has said that Marianne Moore spent years working on an introduction to *Monsieur Teste* for the Bollingen Foundation, and it was not published then only because the poet was not satisfied with the piece.[1]

Valéry's concerns were close to those of Marianne Moore, for whom the mind was a place of continuous struggle, and a center for "the love of doing hard things." The theme of struggle is found throughout her writing, and appears in "Radical" (1919), a remarkable poem that should not have been abandoned after its publication in *Observations* (1924). The poem reads as follows:

RADICAL

Tapering
to a point, conserving everything,
   this carrot is predestined to be thick.
    The world is
     but a circumstance, a mis-
       erable corn-patch for its feet. With ambition, im-
        agination, outgrowth,

nutriment,
with everything crammed belligerent-
   ly inside itself, its fibres breed mon-
    opoly—
     a tail-like, wedge-shaped engine with the
      secret of expansion, fused with intensive heat to
      color of the set-

ting sun and
stiff. For the man in the straw hat, standing still and turning to look back at it,
    as much as
    to say my happiest moment has
      been funereal in comparison with this, the condi-
      tions of life pre-

determined
slavery to be easy, inclined
   away from progress, and freedom, hard. For
    it? Dismiss
    agrarian lore; it tells him this:
      that which it is impossible to force, it is impossible
      to hinder.

                           (O, 48)[2]

"Radical" is one of the few early transitional poems that has neither the earlier "seeing" speaker, conspicuously referred to as "I" and addressing an imaginary listener, nor the later form of self-

address, in which the mind seizes a problem and brings it to consciousness. It does exemplify, however, the poet's meditative practice of taking hold of the object as the first step in illuminating a
human concept.

The images of the carrot and of the human being observing it,
both embodying freedom, illuminate one another as well as the
concept they incarnate. As the carrot is "predestined" to grow, the
man's life is "predetermined," and we are directed to hear the echo
of the one word as we contemplate the other object; however, while
the carrot is committed to its destiny of progress, the man is con-
demned to make an anxious decision between idle enslavement and
the struggle to be free.

In Marianne Moore's poems there is seldom a choice: Dignity and
freedom are attained through hardship, and wisdom results from the
struggle of consciousness. In letters to E. McKnight Kauffer, an
artist with whom she shared her love of Valéry's work, she wrote of
her belief, despite affliction and suffering, in "anastasis—the going
forward." In a letter of 1952 she wrote to Kauffer: "We have the
conviction . . . that one can live in peace in turmoil—like a certain
pond fed by springs only seen in winter in the hard season."[3] Those
letters to Kauffer followed the death of Marianne Moore's mother in
1947, an event that caused her great sorrow; nevertheless, the poet
had concentrated on progress through hardship from the beginning
of her writing career, and hardship was, for her, inner turmoil.

Central to her poetry of the mind's inward growth is her use of
metamorphic imagery that accentuates the tendency of consciousness to pivot continuously from one vivid figure to another. Her
vision of a shifting reality is a further indication of her sense of the
age, whose leading philosophers have questioned the accuracy of
unchanging reality. "What is more precise than precision? Illusion,"
exclaims the speaker of "Armor's Undermining Modesty" (1950), in
what could be a maxim for the twentieth-century view that what we
perceive to be real is not actual, and that optical illusion is the rule,
rather than the exception.

Metamorphic images, then, are used to embody the shifting process of the mind in its encounter with modern reality. Metamorphosis is the function of the poet, who creates what is real by
defining it in terms of changes he perceives. To elucidate this proc-

ess of change, Marianne Moore does not rely on standard meta-morphic myths such as Daphne, Proteus, or Ariel, but on objects from the world around her that move as they are perceived.

Metamorphosis makes its appearance in her poetry in two distinct ways. The first recalls her training in science at Bryn Mawr and its effects on her writing. Images of water, fire and rock—those classic elements of metamorphosis—abound in her poetry, often accom-panying moments of change.

In "Efforts of Affection" (1948), we learn:

> Truly as the sun
> can rot or mend, love can make one
> bestial or make a beast a man.
> (CPMM, 147)

To the scientist, metamorphosis means a change in form without a change in substance. The sun is metamorphic because, as the source of all energy, it is the instigator of change. Fire incessantly changes form and water becomes ice, steam or vapor, just as seas alter from turbulence to calm. Rocks are metamorphic in that the geologic definition of metamorphosis is a change in the form of rock, usually affected by the other elements of heat and water.

Another form of metamorphosis is in the way images are moved for the effect of magical change. In "Spenser's Ireland" (1941) we learn that the country "has not altered" but might if "there be fern seed for unlearn- / ing obduracy and for reinstating / the enchant-ment" (CPMM, 112).

The speaker speculates on Irish obduracy, a characteristic that is "positive" in the poet's polarity between certainty and change, and realizes that if they are stubborn, they also have the power to be

> like enchanted Earl Gerald who
> changed himself into a stag, to
> a great green-eyed cat of
> the mountain.
> (CPMM, 113)

Implicit in Marianne Moore's imagery patterns is a vision that involves the whole of the sensibility and hence the changing relationship of things. Her method of using successive images to enact a process of change recalls Ezra Pound's lines of metamorphosis in Canto V:

> Air, fire, the pale soft light.
> Topaz I manage, and three sorts of blue;
> but on the barb of time.
> The fire? always, and the vision always,
> Ear dull, perhaps, with the vision, flitting
> And fading at will. Weaving with points of gold,
> Gold-yellow, saffron. . . .[4]

Here the poet's way of transcending time is by interweaving the elements. Although the imagery of fire and light is actually built on the Platonic concept of translucence, it presents as well the idea of metamorphosis in the modern age. By its use, the poet relates self-discovery to his vision of the alterable nature of matter.

The aesthetic and psychological implications of Marianne Moore's concept of perceptual change are found in Ezra Pound's definition of the image in "A Few Don'ts by an Imagiste":

> An "Image" is that which presents an intellectual and emotional complex in an instant of time. I use the term "complex" rather in the technical sense employed by the new psychologists, such as Hart. . . .
> It is the presentation of such a "complex" instantaneously which gives that sense of sudden liberation; that sense of freedom from time limits and space limits; that sense of sudden growth, which we experience in the presence of the greatest works of art.[5]

We find in Marianne Moore's poetry images of "sudden growth" working in accordance with those shifts in tone that set into motion the formal and inner debates that structure her poetry of engagement. In the early poems that are rhetorical conversations and "metaphysical" arguments, insights are presented in images treated for their metamorphic properties. For example, at the end of "To Military Progress" (1915), the speaker sees that the savagery of modern destruction will continue ". . . till the evening sky's / red"

(CPMM, 82). In the poem that appeared in 1916 and was retitled "To a Chameleon"[6] (CPMM, 179), the creature's transformation is presented in the metamorphic image of fire, and this change corresponds to a shift in the speaker's thought process. The poem is divided almost precisely in two by a full stop, which determines the leap in thought. In the first sentence the speaker observes a chameleon winding itself around a grapevine, concealed by foliage. At the beginning of the second there is a shift from the rhetoric of direct address to the impersonal tone: the speaker contemplates firelight reflected by a jewel ("Fire laid upon / an emerald") and concludes, again in the tone of direct address, that even this could not transform itself into the colors that the chameleon assumes. When this poem was revised for inclusion in *O to Be a Dragon* (1959), the typographic pattern of the poem was altered to resemble the winding shape of the chameleon. Although the typography has its impact only after the poem has been read, the thought-picture, in addition to supporting the vivid depiction of the image, embodies the creature perceptually and as a continuous process in time.

"Sun" is a remarkable poem that evolved through a fifty-one-year span of revision, finally settling in the poet's seventy-ninth year. First published as "Sun!" in *Contemporary Verse* in 1916, it went through five published variants until it appeared in *Tell Me, Tell Me* and was reprinted in *Complete Poems.*[7]

The central figure of "Sun" is an extended image, exploited to display the argument. Its metamorphic treatment supports the discursive structure. In this poem, which Marianne Moore has cited as an example of her poetic impulse to argue with an idea, the sun incarnates a vision that transforms the image of death in the opening quotation: "No man may him hyde / From Deth holow-eyed." The speaker contemplates the "adverse idea" and finds it inadequate for two human beings: "For us, this inconvenient truth does not suffice." In this third line there is a shift from the incisive tone of the opening aphorism to elegant conversation: the "us" connotes an intimate, rather than a public, use of the third person plural.

Next, there is a shift to illustration: "You are not male or female, but a plan / deep-set within the heart of man." The shift to "you" is typical of the early rhetorical conversations, in which the speaker suddenly addresses the figure or concept of the title.

The sixth and seventh lines of stanza one are expanded for an elaboration of the image, and the following two are contracted for a new assertion:

> Splendid with splendor hid you come, from your Arab abode,
> a fiery topaz smothered in the hand of a great prince who rode
> before you, Sun—whom you outran,
> piercing his caravan.

In the first positive statement of the poem (following two negative assertions), the sun is developed as an image of transformation. Hidden in the description of the sun are phrases that refer back to the figure of "Deth": While " 'No man may him hyde / From Deth holow-eyed,' " the sun, by contrast, arrives "Splendid with splendor *hid*." The figure of the "great prince" is treated as an extension of "Fear" (in the epigraph) and "Deth" (in line two) in being given active, moving properties (it rides, while "Fear accosts" and "deth" approaches). Because both "Fear" and "Deth" are presented as threats to man, "the great prince" is as well, by implication. In line seven "the great prince" is overtaken suddenly by the concept of sun, its caravan pierced.

This metamorphic process continues in the second stanza:

> O Sun, you shall stay
> with us; holiday,
> consuming wrath, be wound in a device
> of Moorish gorgeousness, round glasses spun
> to flame as hemispheres of one
> great hour-glass dwindling to a stem.

The opening lines of stanza two present an argument with the form, as well as the idea, of the opening quotation. There "Deth" is displayed as being inescapable; here, the sun is omnipresent. However, the poet transforms, rather than refutes, the opening aphorism, accomplishing this by referring back to it in rhythm, tone and sound effects. Both stanzas begin with assertions in Skeltonic verse, full lines of accentual verse divided in two. The effect is simultaneously archaic and ironic. In the first stanza the word order is inverted for rhyme, and an unnatural stress falls on "holow-eyed." In the second accents and pauses conform to the conversational phrase. Central to the transforming process are the sound effects: although the first lines of stanza two constitute a contrary idea, their sounds echo those of the opening quotation (the assonance of "O Sun" and "No man," and of "holiday" and "holow-eyed"). In addition, "man" occurs twice in stanza one, and is emphasized by rhyme with "plan," and by light rhyme with "outran" and "caravan." In stanza two "Sun" is presented as the second word (like "man" in stanza one), and is emphasized by the rhymes "spun" and "one," and by the light rhyme, "outrun."

By the end of the second line of stanza two, the sun has been identified as a transforming image, one that is closely identified with man. In the lines that follow, the sun is treated as a unifying metaphor that links the opposed images of "holiday" and "consuming wrath" ("day of wrath" in an earlier version, an image in which the dialectic is more apparent), and is commanded to "consume hostility."

The sun is presented as a visionary figure, on a level of perception deeper than logic or comparison. The sun arrives as hidden fire ("Splendid with splendor hid," "a fiery topaz smothered"), radiant for its disguised radiance, and changes for a visible, active force in relation to the great prince ("whom you outran, / piercing his caravan"). Fire and man are equated in the poem, for the sun, which is addressed directly as "you," replaces the human figure to become the central image. The transforming power of the sun, which is like that of the imagination, is embodied in the technique of referring back to words or images in previous lines.

The movement of the central image of "Sun" ("you come," "you outran," "you shall stay") is determined by successive perceptual discoveries, in addition to the logical sequence of thought. The final lines of the poem construct a new perception based on the metamorphic properties of the central image: "Insurgent feet shall not outrun / multiplied flames, O Sun." The sense of the line refers us back to "outran," the sun's action in the first stanza. "O Sun," the opening of stanza two, refers back to "no man," preparing us for a new image of man by transforming the fearful creature of the opening lines. The sun's dialectical properties are adverted to in its fusion of opposites ("holiday" and "consuming wrath"). Finally, the typographic pattern, which was altered in 1961 to the shape of an hourglass, has a transforming effect. It points up the vividness of the hourglass conceit, supporting the idea of the sun as a unifier of opposites and as a continuous process in time. The sun, then, is the transforming principle of the imagination, which moves through a series of perceptual changes and turns a vision of fear into a vision of hope.

Dominating Marianne Moore's poetry of the twenties are meta-morphic images of the sea, fire, and rock. They are presented as changing in relation to one another as the eye moves over them. Initially, when the dramatic situation of the "I" and the "you" begins to disappear from her work, metamorphic images are used to propel the poems forward, either by themselves or in league with the self-corrective shifts that replace the earlier, discursive changes in tone.

In "The Fish" (1918), the sea, sun, and rock are set in opposition to each other, acted and acting upon as they are watched by an unob-trusive perceiver. The sun penetrates and is fractured: it illuminates the sea, through which fish "wade" (are hindered) and in which barnacles cannot hide; its rays are "split like spun / glass" because of the motion of rock. The water, penetrated by sun, "drives a wedge / of iron through the iron edge" of the cliff (CPMM, 32). Only the rock, scarred though it is by the sea and by the other elements, does not deteriorate because it can survive "on what cannot revive its youth. The sea grows old in it." Although sight is not explicitly named here, as it is named in more than seventy poems after 1921, the eye transforms each object through careful analysis, and the events are presented in continuous motion.

In "Novices" (1923) the transforming power of art is seen as a kind of change that is permanent, drawn in metamorphic imagery and contrasted with change that is superficial, such as fashion. The fashionable literary pretenders of the title are depicted as creatures of change (". . . Acquiring at thirty what at sixty they will be trying to forget") who are unseeing beings ("blind to the right word, deaf to satire") and are bored by " 'the detailless perspective of the sea' " (CPMM, 61). In contrast, "the Hebrew language," an embodiment of ideal language and art, is discovered to be a more compelling kind of change, "this drama of water against rocks":

"an abyss of verbs full of reverberations and tempestuous
                                      energy"

in which action perpetuates action and angle is at variance
                                                    with angle
till submerged by the general action; . . .

                                                    (CPMM, 61)

A shift from light to fire corresponds to a shift from the super-
ficiality of the half-writers to the depths of "the Hebrew language."
The "novices" are presented in images of light and of surfaces: "they
present themselves as a contrast to sea-serpented regions 'unlit by
the half-lights of more conscious art,'" and they are "Accustomed
to the recurring phosphorescence of antiquity" and to "the lucid
movements of the royal yacht" in calm water.

Light breaks through to fire in the presentation of "the Hebrew
language"

    with its "great livid stains like long slabs of green marble,"
    its "flashing lances of perpendicular lightning" and "molten
                                            fires swallowed up,"
    "with foam on its barriers,"
    "crashing itself out in one long hiss of spray."

                                                    (CPMM, 61)

This is a scientific instance of metamorphosis in that the wave
gathers its force and expends itself by harnessing the sun's energy,
which is the source of all change. The movement approximates
human thought in that the pattern of the mind is characterized by
the changes in the structure of fire. In the poem the mind moves
through to a perception of the genuine in art and in man by focusing
on idealized language, which is, paradoxically, permanent in its
capacity to transform itself.

In "An Octopus" (1924) the forms of elements fluctuate under
inquisitive scrutiny: as the eye moves over it, the mountain of the
title transforms its animals and vegetation and is transformed by
them. Changes in water, rock and foliage are presented in ways that
are scientifically correct and mysterious. The mountain changes its
foliage to the extent that trees, hardly recognizable, resemble "dust-
brushes," their branches shrinking in trying to escape "from the
hard mountain 'planed by ice and polished by the wind.'" The rock
is "left at the mercy of the weather; / 'stained traversely by iron

where the water drips down'" (CPMM, 71). In this poem, meta-morphic images—those poetic figures for changes in the forms of natural substances—are used with imagery of sight and with refer-ences to seeing phenomena. Bears are "inspecting unexpectedly / ant-hills and berry bushes" while their den is "concealed in the confusion / of 'blue forests thrown together with marble and jasper and agate'" and a goat's eye is "fixed on the waterfall which never seems to fall— / an endless skein swayed by the wind" (CPMM, 72). Human visitors, eager to see everything, see nothing: the mountain is unchangeable in the face of change ("intact when it is cut"— CPMM, 75), and remote from conventional perception ("damned for its sacrosanct remoteness"—CPMM, 75).

The poet's fusion of metamorphic imagery and perceptual change is fundamental to her aesthetic for engagement, for it culminates in the later poems in imagery that figures forth a way of penetrating confusion that clouds personal attitudes toward conditions and ideas. Her concept of perceiving reality evolves from "Poetry" (1919) to "The Mind Is an Enchanting Thing" (1943). In the earlier poem the speaker distinguishes between the "raw material" of art and "that which is, on the other hand / genuine." The "genuine," like the "Hebrew language" of "Novices" and "Hebrew poetry" of "The Past Is the Present," may infuse and intensify the "raw material" but it may never be achieved because it is idealized, similar to Baudelaire's idealization of the poet and his art.

In the later work the "raw material" and the "genuine" are split apart, as it were, and their dichotomy informs the poet's metamor-phic imagery. Although the subject matter consists of commonplace objects, the structures approximate the precise but fluctuating pro-gressions of consciousness. It is as though the poet seeks to transcend the world she has analyzed, in the transitional period, with "X-ray-like inquisitive intensity" ("People's Surroundings" [1922], CPMM, 57).

In the early work the poet creates a dialectic of perception, em-phasizing the sense in which seeing is not seeing: the elephant speaker of "Melancthon" (1918), for example, claims to see and hear in contrast to man, who is seen and heard, and who "was made / to see and not to see; to hear and not to hear" (CP, 45). In the transi-tional poems the perceptual dialectic is fused with metamorphic images, as in "Marriage" (1923) and "An Octopus" (1924). In "A

Grave" (1921), another poem of this period, there is a subtle perceptual dialectic: "The sea is a collector, quick to return a rapacious
look" (CPMM, 49). Here, the sea is treated as a subject as well as for
its homonym, "see," and the word "look" is used as subject and
object in the sense that a look is given and a look is worn. In the
later poetry animals and objects become screens on which the poet
focuses consciousness.

"The Mind Is an Enchanting Thing" (1943) incarnates a process of
psychic change as a way of perceiving reality in the modern world.
First, it contains the associative connections, self-corrections, leaps
and other devices that approximate consciousness, enabling the
poet to maintain a tension between the object she contemplates and
worldly matters or ideas. Second, the poet's imagery consists of the
"raw material" of the world around her, but she uses this imagery in
ways that capture the continuously moving, transforming techniques of the mind (CPMM, 134).

In a group of poems of the thirties and forties, the poet assimilates
consciousness by using images of transformation, and by presenting
the animals and objects that capture her fancy as creatures that
change before the eyes. They may assume different forms or may
alter from visibility to invisibility, hence they embody the dialectic
of human vision and the process of perceptual change.

Although the subject of "The Jerboa" (1932), a freeborn desert rat,
is described in vivid detail, it has magical characteristics as well: it
makes "fern-seed / footprints" (CPMM, 15). Fern seeds, an image
that occurs frequently in the later poetry, are spores once thought to
be seeds and were believed to have the power of making one invisible. The jerboa bewitches its aggressor and assumes different propor-
tions and colors:

                                        Course

          the jerboa, or
        plunder its food store,
            and you will be cursed. It
            honors the sand by assuming its color;
                closed upper paws seeming one with the fur
                in its flight from a danger.
                                        (CPMM, 14)

In "The Plumet Basilisk" (1933) the life and hope of America are contained in the changing figure of the title, a lizard whose ability to transform itself and to become invisible have enabled it to survive. The lizard's change is fused with the metamorphic image of fire: it is presented in imagery that moves from the green of "blazing driftwood" to the colors of "fire opal" to "the living firework" (CPMM, 20). Water, another metamorphic image, is related to the amphibious lizard's ability to swim, demonstrating "mythology's wish / to be interchangeably man and fish" (CPMM, 23). The lizard embodies the water, land and air of a country the exploiting Spaniards failed to find because of its ability to evade the eye:

> the innocent, rare, gold-
> defending dragon that as you look begins to be a
> nervous naked sword on little feet, with threefold
> separate flame above the hilt, inhabiting
>
> fire eating into air.
>
>   (CPMM, 23–24)

Change is simultaneously godlike and subhuman in "Half Deity," which first appeared in 1935, was collected only in *The Pangolin* and *What Are Years* and then was abandoned. "Half Deity, / half worm," comprising the title and first line, describes the ambivalent butterfly that is the central image of this poem. The creature is characterized in terms of perceptual change, metamorphosis, and self-contradictory images, called a "historic metamorphoser," a "blind / all-seeing butterfly," and depicted with "eyes staring skyward and chest arching / bravely out." The butterfly changes its definition as the speaker observes it, becoming an "unwormlike unteachable butterfly- / zebra" (WY, 17–19).

In "The Pangolin" (1936) the anteater of the title is the focal center of the poet's thoughts, affording the means by which she works through to a new definition of man. Although the animal's exemplary virtues are given in the poem (it is nonaggressive, graceful, a model of exactness), they are presented in a form that approximates thought. The poem opens with a sentence fragment whose disjointedness signifies reflection: "Another armored animal—scale lapping scale with spruce-cone regularity." The device of self-correction is used to introduce observations about the closing sense organs ("the closing earridge— / or bare ear"). There are contradictions, too, in the imagery that is used to present these organs ("contracting nose and eye apertures / impenetrably closeable"— CPMM, 117).

The device of self-correction is also fused with the metamorphic image of the moon. In the second stanza the anteater is described as a night creature, "stepping in the moonlight, / on the moonlight peculiarly" that it may preserve the strength of its claws and wear only the outer edges of its hands. Repetition is fused with metamorphic imagery in the heightened exclamation ending stanza three:

> Sun and moon and day and night and man and beast
>> each with a splendor
>>> which man in all his vileness cannot
>>> set aside; each with an excellence!
>>>>> (CPMM, 118)

In a subtle way the poet is working through to the idea that the pangolin, a night creature, is not a seeing animal. The true subject of this poem is man as a seeing being. The emphasis on man becomes apparent in the penultimate stanza, with its shift in tone: "Bedizened or stark / naked, man, the self, the being we call human" (CPMM, 119). When man is described as being unafraid yet fearing ("Not afraid of anything is he / and then goes cowering forth"), we recall that the pangolin is " 'fearful yet to be feared.' " The pangolin, for all its virtues, is hampered by consistency; man, on the other hand, is characterized by contradictions and opposites, and this very inconsistency is his greatness. He is consistent only with the "formula": "warm blood, no gills, two pairs of hands and a few hairs— that is a mammal." In the final lines the emergent vision of man is accompanied by a metamorphic image of the sun, in which the poet adverts to its power to generate energy that produces change:

> The prey of fear, he, always
>> curtailed, extinguished, thwarted by the dusk, work
>>>> partly done,
>> says to the alternating blaze,
>> "Again the sun!

anew each day; and new and new and new,
that comes into and steadies my soul."
(CPMM, 120)

The poetic rightness of this passage is in the way the language
enacts the fusion of the experiential aspect of things and the inner
vision, and this fusion is supported by the poet's adherence to the
actual progression of thought. The poem moves from idea to radiant
image in a process that Freud tells us is characteristic of the unconscious: in nearly all dreams, he writes, thoughts are transformed
into visual images. Further, the union of man and anteater suggests
that dream technique of combining two or more persons so that a
new image emerges. As Freud states:

> In composition, where this is extended to persons, the dream-
> image contains features which are peculiar to one or the other
> of the persons concerned but not common to them; so that the
> combination of these features leads to the appearance of a new
> unity, a composite figure.[8]

The poet has created a new human image by means of the form that
imitates consciousness. Aside from the approximation of thought
and of economy which characterize the unconscious as well as poetic
speech, the use of these devices enables the poet to contemplate man
while ostensibly focusing on the animal. The transformation of
thought to visual image and the use of composite dream persons are
further aids to this process.

In addition, the poet assimilates the mental process of referring
back to previous images and transforming them. The concluding
passage quoted above, depicting man, recalls the description of the
pangolin in its like images used in opposite ways. Man is "cur-
tailed" (limited), a word whose etymologic meaning (tail cut) contains a pun: man, being tailless, is inferior to the pangolin in that he
lacks the animal's graceful tail, used as a tool. Further, man is
"extinguished," recalling in an inverse way the pangolin's impene-
trable armor. Man is "thwarted by dusk," calling back the pangolin's solitary trips at night.

One of the most striking effects of this passage, though, is the way
in which techniques of the unconscious are used not only as form

but as theme, contributing to the concluding picture of man. Man
thrives on change ("the alternating blaze") and on repetition ("and
new and new and new"), and on the struggle between alternating
images. We recall that the pangolin is compelled to shut out "sun
and moon and day and night," leaving his nest only after nightfall.
Man, on the other hand, finding strength in the very intensity of his
frustration, lives on fluctuation and light. Man's limitations, then,
are his potential excellence: The blazing, alternating image of the
sun, and the transformation of day and night give us the rhythm of
tragedy as well as of consciousness.

"The Mind Is an Enchanting Thing" (1943) begins with a commonplace that is rescued from banality by the second line. The
variation of "Enchanting" / "enchanted" within the parallel construction enriches the word by intensifying the meaning. "Enchanting," the present participial adjective, in this context, means "to be
charming" or "to be fascinating," and has a flat connotation when it
occurs in ordinary speech. "Enchanted," the past participial adjective, means "to be enraptured"; hence, the two lines, juxtaposed,
characterize the mind as an ordinary thing that is under an extraordinary power. The contrast of "Enchanting" / "enchanted" also
prepares the reader for two kinds of motion found throughout the
poem: that which moves and that which is moved. And, after one
reads the poem closely, a third meaning emerges: the mind is the
poet and poetry.

Although the tone of the combination title and first line is conversational, we hear the diction of thought by the end of the second line
because of the absence of transition between the two thoughts (the
mind is enchanting because it is enchanted). At this point the
speaker is not the poet as conversationalist but the poet as thinker,
mumbling aloud to achieve precision. In the first stanza the mind's
rapid association is likened to "the glaze on a / katydid-wing" and
"Gieseking playing Scarlatti" (CPMM, 134), images that are linked
by their quick darting movement and by rhyme ("wing," "Gieseking," "playing"). The internal rhyme is richly intricate: "ing" is
repeated five times in the first stanza.

The mind's tentative way of moving through, as to an idea, is
likened to the activity of a quick, airy object ("haired feathers").
However, their likeness is contradicted by rhythm and sound. The
high vowel sounds of the preceding stanza ("katydid-wing," "Giese-

king") modulate to the deeper vowel sounds in the last two lines of the passage quoted above ("though," "walks along," "ground"); in contrast to the light rhymes in the preceding stanza ("sun," "legion"), there is consonantal dissonance ("mind," "ground") at the end of stanza two. In addition, the second stanza ends with the first full stop in the poem, creating a definite pause, and making the movement of the mind sound definite, plodding and firm.

The contrast here resembles the process Freud has named condensation, the technique of combining contradictory thoughts as though no contradiction exists. Like most of the argumentative tendencies of thought, however, this technique aids, rather than hinders, progression. The result of the condensation here is, I believe, that the mind derives freedom from contradictory impulses, and can be either tentative and quick (like "haired feathers") or definite and plodding, as the sounds in the last two lines of stanza two indicate.

In stanza three it appears that perception is the result of another contradiction. "Not hearing" can be "hearing":

> It has memory's ear
> that can hear without
> having to hear.

The mind, we learn later, "is memory's eye; / it's conscientious inconsistency." Perception is the result of the mind's tendency to change a thing into something else, not so much by contradiction as by self-correction; "conscientious inconsistency" implies a process of transformation, rather than contradiction. The process is best illustrated by the remarkable conceit of the gyroscope in stanza three:

> Like the gyroscope's fall,
> truly unequivocal
> because trued by regnant certainty,
>
> it is a power of
> strong enchantment.

Like Donne's image of the compasses in "A Valediction: Forbidding Mourning," the dissimilarity of mind and gyroscope is as engaging as the similarity. However, the difference between the two conceits is basic to Marianne Moore's method. In Donne's comparison there is a gap between the physical and the metaphysical: the comparison of "stiffe twin compasses" and lovers' souls is as distant as it is right—and that is the point. Marianne Moore's comparison, on the other hand, is precisely right: The spinning mind tilts just as the gyroscope tilts as it veers from gravity, having the power to right itself in motion. This precision becomes, paradoxically, the magical transforming force of the mind and of poetry. The meaning of "enchantment" here is the "power to transport," the creative power. The intensity of the mind's capacity to transport is heightened by the force of the words "power" and "strong," and reinforced by the variations of the verb "to enchant." Enchantment, the power of the mind and of art, is the mysterious capacity for perceptual change. It is the transforming process of becoming aware, which is fundamental to poetry.

Stanza six, the climax of the poem, reveals the process of "enchantment":

> It tears off the veil; tears
>   the temptation, the
> mist the heart wears,
>   from its eyes—if the heart
>   has a face; . . .
>   (CPMM, 134–35)

In the preceding lines the mind is described as "memory's eye" and "conscientious inconsistency," and the climax illustrates that process. The "veil," or blindness, is torn off along with the heart's "mist," and these two qualities are not examined for their respective merits. They are presented in a parallel construction with the object changed in each clause. The construction serves the tone of self-correction, and the "if" reinforces the tone, embodying the mind's effort to attain precision. A gloss on the meaning is found in lines from "Style" (1956): "it is like the eyes / or say the face, of Palestrina by El Greco" (CPMM, 170). In "The Mind Is an Enchanting Thing" the mind achieves the power to *see itself.*

After the climax two of the images presented earlier as similes become metaphors. Previously, the mind had been likened to "Gieseking playing Scarlatti." This image is transformed to fire in the "inconsistencies / of Scarlatti." The simile

                        It

        is like the dove-
                    neck animated by
        sun

is transformed, after the climax, to "It's fire in the dove-neck's / iridescence" (CPMM, 134, 135).

Here, as in "In Distrust of Merits," the poet fuses metamorphic imagery and perceptual change. In "In Distrust of Merits," the poet emphasizes the metamorphic properties of rock and water, linking them with vision:

                    the mountainous
        wave makes us who look, know

            depth.
                        (CPMM, 136)

Here, the metamorphic image of fire is the source of the mind's change. As the sun, which has played over the images early in the poem, breaks through to fire, the similes become metaphors. The mind has the power to impose order ("Gieseking playing Scarlatti") and to become those luminous and changing things ("iridescence" and "inconsistencies") it encounters.

All of the imagery here is paired with a contrary. The moving "wing" is moved by sun; the ear of memory "can hear without / having to hear"; Gieseking plays Scarlatti and Scarlatti presents inconsistencies; the "dove-neck" is "animated by / sun" and emits iridescence; the "veil" is both "temptation" and "mist." "Unconfusion" is the result of "confusion" submitted to proof, a paradox pointing up the mind's power to achieve clarity by seeing through a maze of contradictions. The concluding statement, "it's / not a Herod's oath that cannot change," with its double negative, enacts the mind's change in its struggle between contradictory ideas and images.

The image of fire at the close of the poem is in a sense spiritually perceived, resembling some of the images of the French Symbolists. However, in terms of the structure of the poem, the true impact of this image arises out of its psychological accuracy. Fire is an instance of metamorphosis, which characterizes perceptual change. Fire is the source of the contradictions at the close of the poem, and contradiction is the law of the unconscious. In the theme and structure of the poem, contradiction is progress, which also characterizes the mind. In response to irregular details the mind formulates opposing laws, and this dialectic becomes the basis of learning: repression and its aid to learning is an example of how the mind moves forward by containing opposites.

If change defines the mind, it characterizes the creative process as well. The mind's "change" in the concluding statement echoes the sounds of "enchanting," "enchanted," "enchantment," a recurrence that has the poetic function of rhyme and the psychic implication of progress by repetition. The repetition of sound here also evokes the three meanings of the key verb "to enchant" as it has been used heretofore ("Enchanting": fascinating; "enchanted": enraptured; "enchantment": power to transport). The changes rung on the verb suggest its root meaning as well: "to sing" (*cantare*). A gloss on the meaning of mind can be found in "The Mind, Intractable Thing" (1965), in which the poet describes the mind as having "made wordcraft irresistible" (CPMM, 208). In the poem the "mind," then, is "the power of song" or "the power to sing," which is here—as it is throughout the poetry of Marianne Moore—the result of growth by perceptual change.

V

"A Quite New Rhythm":
The Spoken Art
of Marianne Moore's Poetry

"A quite new rhythm" was T. S. Eliot's response to Marianne Moore's poetry in 1923, and there is hardly a better way to describe the compelling power of her cadences.[1] There are, however, methods of versification that bear considering because they are essential to her poetry of engagement.

In keeping with the form of argumentation that evolved, as we have seen, from her beginnings as a writer, the poetry of Marianne Moore is a spoken art. The primary aesthetic effect of any of her poems is what we hear, and what we hear is the voice of the person who sees, remembers, and changes. The evolution of rhythm in her poetry is a gradual mastery of naturalness gained, paradoxically, through organizing devices that are highly complex. To achieve the conversational ease, her rhythmic methods grow progressively intricate over the years.

Rhythmic divisions of the early structures correspond to rhetorical shifts that are in the metaphysical tradition of "passionate, paradoxical reasoning," to use Sir Herbert Grierson's term; in some of the poems composed from 1916 through 1918, rhythmic devices reinforce the levels of a dialectic in which images used to embody principles are presented vividly and later contradicted. Rhythmic structures of the later poetry follow the gradual evolution of an inner dialectic whose shifts approximate the contradictions of consciousness.

Built on the rhetorical figures of argumentation (assertion, amplification, climactic statement, concluding statement, as well as negative assertion, "correction," rhetorical question), the poems are divided accordingly into two or more related parts. Typical poems are arranged in two sections, one rhythmically a close approximation of the other, or into several sections that include at least one rhythmic pair. The two-part poem usually is based on a juxtaposition of polarities or a balance of images (roughly analogous to the hokku and the sonnet); the structure of several parts is divided according to levels of discourse. Rhythmic effects of the later poetry embody a tension between the world and the object on which the poet's mind has focused.

It is a commonplace of Marianne Moore criticism before 1965 that the poet found discipline for her freer forms by writing syllabic verse, in which the line lengths of a repeated stanzaic pattern are determined by the numbers of syllables, rather than stresses. This criticism has centered on the visual arrangement of lines on the page.[2] Later, critics began to relate the typographic pattern to what is heard when the poem is spoken, which is directed with more accuracy to the poet's concern: Charles Tomlinson, for example, wrote in 1969 that syllabic control enables her to "make available to verse the material and cadences of prose speech and prose writing."[3]

There is no doubt that syllabic stanzaic patterns exist in many of the poems of Marianne Moore and, further, that the method is deliberate, because the number of syllables in a line is inaudible in English, which is a stressed language. The poet was more conscious of syllabic prosody in the earlier poems than in the later, when the practice of counting the numbers of syllables in lines gradually enabled her to hear them without adding. On the other hand, there are good reasons for questioning syllabic prosody as a dominant element in the poetry's rhythm. First, she increasingly revised stanzaic patterns to avoid unnatural word divisions, and second, late in her life Marianne Moore expressed her unequivocal dislike for the term. The third reason, which is essential to understanding her achievement, is that syllabic prosody does not account for the impact of her cadences; rather, it exists as a frame for what is heard when the poem is spoken aloud.

In 1941 and again in 1950 Marianne Moore wrote of her stanzaic patterns. Laurence Stapleton has quoted the poet's note in an anthology about stanzas "identical in number of syllables and rhyme plan, with the first stanza.[4] In 1950 she wrote in a letter to a student, Thomas P. Murphy, "I write in rhymed stanzas, each identical with the other in pattern. . . ."[5]

She seldom spoke of patterned stanzas after that, however, and in her interview with Donald Hall in 1960, Marianne Moore replied to his questions about syllabic verse, "I never 'plan' a stanza."[6] In 1967 she told me that she repudiated syllabics as a "method" and as a basis for her verse. She affirmed that her first concern was for the spoken pattern, and for the effects that are heard when the poem is read aloud. Her aim, she said, was to make the poetry sound natural, and to achieve a progressive continuous movement from the first line to the last. Further, her indication that the punctuation, rather than the line ending, determines the vocal unit and the pause, tells us that conversational phrases, rather than lines, are the poetry's true rhythmic divisions.[7]

Marianne Moore's disavowal of syllabic verse did not represent a change in her beliefs. Her explicit denial of this method came late in her career only because critical emphasis made her realize that her regard for visual symmetry led readers to emphasize its importance. She had always concentrated on spoken rhythm, whether or not she made the visual pattern draw readers' eyes to what she would have them hear. As early as 1914 she wrote, in "Feeling and Precision," that one of her aids to composition was to break a longer sentence that seemed obscure into shorter units "by imagining into what phrases it would fall as conversation" (P, 3). And in 1916 she wrote, in "The Accented Syllable": "By the tone of voice I mean that intonation in which the accents which are responsible for it are so unequivocal as to persist, no matter under what circumstances the syllables are read or by whom they are read. . . ."[8] Although speech divisions are the units of composition in all of her work, and punctuation, rather than line or stanza, determines the writing unit, line lengths have a more important function in the later poetry. In "No Swan So Fine" (1932) and in "The Paper Nautilus" (1940), for example, shorter lines correspond to vocal units.

Marianne Moore did affirm, in 1967, that her method of composition changed in the thirties, after she heard her voice reading the poems on records for the first time. It was in that decade that the spoken pattern became of chief importance to her. After this, she undertook years of revision:

At first, I never realized until we got tape recorders and records that the spoken line is different from the one on the page sometimes. And then I tried to read out loud what I'd written, and then I saw I would have to alter a good deal. Some of the lines wouldn't read, and I revised a number of things. I found that in reading a thing aloud you have to change the wording.[9]

Although the rhythmic effects of her poetry were always in keeping with her concern for spoken form, certain visual features of later poems and revisions direct the eye to what the ear perceives. Her increasing attention to the line as vocal unit and her use of fewer hyphenated words at line endings are among the practices that resulted in her realization of the effects of reading poems aloud.

Revisions startled many of Marianne Moore's readers when the *Complete Poems* first appeared in 1967. (The dramatic reduction of "Poetry" to three lines and the omission of many fine poems from the collection were disconcerting as well, but those are other matters.) As for revisions, poems she altered for spoken effects, and whose free variants appear in this edition, are "Picking and Choosing" (1920), "England" (1920), and "Peter" (1923). Other free variants in the *Complete Poems* had been published in earlier volumes and in journals: The free version of "When I Buy Pictures" (1921) appeared in the *Dial* with the virtually simultaneous appearance of its syllabic counterpart in *Poems*,[10] and the free variant of "The Student" (1932) first appeared in *What Are Years* (1941). The original stanzaic arrangements of "Picking and Choosing" and "Peter" were replaced by free verse patterns whose line endings correspond to breath pauses. For example, the first published version of "Peter" contained the following passage:

> Profound sleep is
> not with him, a fixed illusion. Springing about with
> froglike ac-
>
> curacy, emitting jerky cries when taken in the hand, he is
> himself
> again; to sit caged by the rungs of a domestic chair would
> be unprofit-

able—human. What is the good of hypocrisy? It
  is permissible to choose one's employment, to abandon
    the wire nail, the
        roly-poly, when it shows signs of being no longer
        a pleas-

ure, to score the adjacent magazine with a double line of
  strokes.

(O, 52)

The corresponding passage of the revised "Peter" reads:

Profound sleep is not with him a fixed illusion.
Springing about with froglike accuracy, with jerky cries
when taken in hand, he is himself again;
to sit caged by the rungs of a domestic chair
would be unprofitable—human. What is the good of
                         hypocrisy?
It is permissible to choose one's employment,
to abandon the nail, or roly-poly,
when it shows signs of being no longer a pleasure. . . .

(CPMM, 43)

In the first passage the number of syllables in each line corresponds to those in succeeding stanzas. The second passage is typical of her revisions from stanzaic to free verse structures. Occasionally, she changed free verse to stanzaic structures, as well.

Obviously, "syllabic verse" is an element in the poetry; it functions primarily as a scaffolding on which to structure the poet's natural, conversational rhythms. However, there are other considerations that contribute to the "quite new rhythm."

Recent critics have explored many kinds of rhythmic devices in modern poetry, in what seems a collective effort either to avoid or to define the term "free verse." For example, Benjamin Hrushovsky, in an article entitled "On Free Rhythms in Modern Poetry," has pointed out that rhythm can be based not only on meter but on "syntagmatic relations, word order, syntactic tensions; repetitions of sound, meaning elements, etc. Practically everything in the written poem can contribute to the shaping of the rhythm."[11] Although his statement applies to meter, rather than to syllabic verse, it is useful in considering the poetry of Marianne Moore as well as modern poetry in general.

As for Marianne Moore, the poet has repeatedly used certain devices such as balanced images, sound concurrences, and grammatical tensions to pattern her "free verse." These techniques are based, I believe, on the style of debate that has evolved throughout her work.

The early poems (from 1907 through summer 1915) involve tensions between contrasting ideas that disciplined the urgent conversational tone, with its normal word order and continuity. Those poems have cadences whose accents are increasingly drawn out by tone and meaning.

The earliest poems of argumentation were divided into two parts, one section rhythmically following the other. The dramatic situation consisted of a speaker and a listener addressed as "I" and "you," and the shift was based on the speaker's negative response to an idea. The two-part division, belonging to the entire poem rather than to the line or the stanza, is found in two poems composed in conventional meter before summer 1915, "Progress" (retitled "I May, I Might, I Must," CPMM, 178) and "That Harp You Play So Well," which the poet abandoned after its initial publication in Poetry (May 1915).[12]

In "I May, I Might, I Must" (see page 45), the "you" and the "I" are presented in either clause of a single complex sentence, which is nearly bisected by the comma following "impassable." "That Harp You Play So Well" is another of the rhetorical conversations divided precisely in two by a shift in the argument: in the first two stanzas the speaker praises King David, the listener within the poem addressed as "you"; in the last two stanzas the speaker argues with the Old Testament figure. The poem begins:

> O David, if I had
> Your power, I should be glad—
>   In harping, with the sling,
>   In patient reasoning!

An argumentative assertion marks the turning point at the beginning of stanza three:

> But, David, if the heart
> Be brass, what boots the art
> Of exorcising wrong,
> Of harping to a song?

In both of these poems certain devices subordinate the effects of line and stanza to the continuous movement of the whole. Although the rhythm of "Progress" is less natural than the straightforward diction, the poet does not force unnatural accents or impede the conversational flow. Although the end rhymes, masculine and perfect, might be expected to induce pauses at line endings, certain sound concurrences belonging to the entire poem (repetitions of "tell" and "I," correspondences of "why" and "try") lessen the impact of line endings and allow the phrase, rather than the line, to determine the pause. The iambic rhythm of "That Harp You Play So Well" has a less natural effect than that of "Progress," occasionally encouraging artificial accents, as in the line "In patient reasoning!" However, certain concurrences of words and sounds in stanzas one and three ("O David" and "But, David"; the corresponding recurrence of "In" and "Of," the repetition of "harping") impart a symmetrical balance that focuses attention on the overall pattern rather than on the relation of lines within stanzas.

During the poet's departure from conventional meter, which took place over a period of eight months beginning in April 1915, her poems contain elements that link freer rhythms to argumentation. In an untitled poem that was later called "The Past Is the Present" (December 1915),[13] whose argument is about free verse, the phrase "I shall revert to you, / Habakkuk," which occurs midway through the poem, marks a shift in the argument. The tension between grammar and meaning in this phrase reinforces the division between the adversary's position and the speaker's answer. The speaker is arguing against those who maintain that a conventional pattern ("external action" and "rhyme") is outworn in modern verse. By using the future tense of a verb meaning to return ("shall revert"), the poet unifies past and future in the figure of Habakkuk, the prophet whose vision was embodied in unrhymed biblical verse.

The earliest of the poems that are not in meter and rhyme are moved forward by rhetorical shifts and are versified by devices that emphasize and link together conversational phrases. One of the

most interesting of these devices is her original use of the caesura
combined with the repetition of similar sounds, often light rhymes.
Basically, the technique is a variant of Old English versification, in
which the first two stressed syllables in a line alliterated with a
third, on the other side of the hemistich.

Because lines are subordinate to phrases in Marianne Moore's
early poetry, the caesura and the recurrence of like sounds are used
to relate parts of poems, rather than parts of lines. In "To Statecraft
Embalmed" (December 1915), the caesura coupled with sound recurrences is used as a patterning device for rhythm that is free:

> transmigrating from the
> sarcophagus, | | you wind
> snow
> silence round us | | and with moribund talk, . . .
> (CPMM, 35)

Here, light rhymes preceding the caesuras ("sarcophagus," "us")
gently set off the conversational phrases they terminate; in addition,
dissonances on either side of the caesura in one line ("round,"
"moribund") unite the two parts of the line and link it to a previous
line by their echo of "wind." Apart from emphasizing the conversational phrase and minimizing the impact of end rhyme, these sound
effects serve the amplification of the image, which is developed in
this passage as the mummified Ibis that represents "statecraft embalmed."

In "Old Tiger" light rhyme is used at the ends of nearly all
conversational phrases, an effect which heightens the discursive
tone. For example, the sound relationships enrich the following
passage, which is a rhetorical amplification of the opening assertion
(phrase endings are marked by vertical lines and sound concurrences
are italicized):

> An exemplary hind leg hang*ing* | like a plummet at the
> end of a
>
> str*ing*— | the tufts of fur depressed like grass
> on which something heavy has been ly*ing*— | nominal
> ears of black glass— |

Another source of rhythmic effects in the early work is the technique of making patterns out of negative constructions and diminishing figures, a device common to Elizabethan and metaphysical
poetry. The formalizing effects of negative statements can be found
in some of the poet's earliest departures from conventional meter.
For example, "To Military Progress" (April 1915) and "To Statecraft
Embalmed" (December 1915) are rhetorical conversations with figures that embody concepts of political ethics. "To Military Progress" begins:

> You use your mind
> like a millstone to grind
>   chaff.
> You polish it
> and with your warped wit
>   laugh
>
> at your torso, . . .
>   (CPMM, 82)

The second poem opens:

> There is nothing to be said for you. Guard
> your secret. Conceal it under your hard
>   plumage, necromancer.
>   O
> bird, whose tents were "awnings of Egyptian
> yarn," shall Justice' faint zigzag inscription—
>   leaning like a dancer—
>   show. . . .
>   (CPMM, 35)

Among the structural characteristics they share are regular end
rhymes and a recurrent monosyllabic line. Their central rhythmic
difference is that the former poem is in conventional meter and the
latter cannot be systematically scanned. "To Military Progress" is in
iambic dimeter alternating with a stressed monosyllabic line, and has
exceptions only in lines five and seven, curiously lines that contain
the "warped wit" and "torso" of the central image. In the freer poem,

"To Statecraft Embalmed," the first nineteen lines (slightly more than half of the entire thirty-two) are composed of negative and affirmative statements and the latter thirteen lines, composed of statements expressed in the affirmative, comprise an ironic disparagement of the concept. In the first part of the poem, statements expressed in the negative contain the words "nothing," "not," or "no": "There is nothing to be said for you," "You say not," "no / virtue in you," "Discreet behavior is not now the sum / of statesmanlike good sense" (CPMM, 35). The negative statements constitute chiding assertions in an argument the speaker is having with the preserved Ibis—a bird venerated in ancient Egypt and entombed with kings—who will not answer the question of whether Justice will make "the pulse of its once vivid sovereignty" known in modern times. But just as the negative assertions convey a growing exasperation with Ibis, the illustrations, stated in the affirmative, betray the speaker's fascination with that royal symbol of wisdom ("whose tents were 'awnings of Egyptian yarn' "). The second half of the poem, in which the negatives disappear, attacks the "dead grace" that the bird's discretion recommends:

> you'll see the wrenched distortion
> of suicidal dreams
> go
> staggering toward itself and with its bill
> attack its own identity, . . .

The function of the negative constructions in terms of the poet's meaning is clearly perceived in the comparison with "To Military Progress." In both, the conceptual image represents a fatal division in man. In the earlier poem the separation of mind and body is scored by a contemptuous speaker; in the later poem it is acted out by a series of subtle shifts in the argument. In that argument the speaker himself is divided between admiration for dead beauty and apprehension of its danger.

Marianne Moore's negative statements also have an exhortatory manner like those of Shakespeare ("Not marble, nor the gilded monuments"), especially in their reinforcement of rhetorical shifts and demarcation of rhythmic divisions. In Shakespeare's Sonnet

116, for example, negative assertions are used to introduce the first quatrain ("Let me not to the marriage of true minds / Admit impediments"), the second quatrain ("O no! It is an ever fixed mark") and the third quatrain ("Love's not Time's fool"), and the couplet is constructed in the negative ("If this be error and upon me proved, / I never writ, nor no man ever loved").

In like manner, Marianne Moore uses negative statements to emphasize rhythmic divisions of poems that are structured in two parts, one section approximating the other in cadence and contradicting the other in meaning. For example, "Sun," a poem examined earlier, is built on two stanzas in which images of death and of life are juxtaposed. The opening quotation and the concluding statement are expressed in the negative: " 'No man may him hyde / From Deth holow-eyed' " and "Insurgent feet shall not outrun / multiplied flames, O Sun" (CPMM, 234). The two negative assertions have an enveloping effect that contribute to the two-part rhythm of the poem. While they are similar in having negative constructions, they are unalike in having opposite meanings, for "Deth" is inescapable in the first, and "Sun," principle of natural life, is inescapable in the last. The repetition of the negative is one of the devices that serves the transformation of the image of "fear" into one of "hope."

In like manner, "You are Like the Realistic Product . . ." (1916, retitled "To a Chameleon") contains a negative statement that reinforces the poem's division in two halves with corresponding cadences and contradictory images. The poem is constructed in two sentences: the first occupying six lines; the second, five. In the first, an affirmative ironic statement, we learn that the chameleon is hidden by foliage; in the second, a negative statement, we find that reflected firelight "could not snap the spectrum up for food / as you have done." The method of distinguishing rhythmically paired stanzas by the negative-affirmative contrast is found even more frequently in the later poems, as in "An Egyptian Pulled Glass Bottle in the Shape of a Fish" and in "No Swan So Fine."

Negative statements are also used as patterning devices in poems that have more than two parts, whose rhythmic divisions correspond to rhetorical shifts. In another poem explored earlier, "Old Tiger," whose rhythmic structure is based (with exceptions) on shorter phrases of assertions in the tone of direct address and longer phrases of illustrations in the tone of formal discourse, many of the assertions are connected in the negative. At the outset the speaker asserts ironically that various inferior animals are "nothing" to the creature of the title. While one of the early climaxes of the poem is a negative assertion pointing up the tiger's apparent superiority to the other animals ("you to whom a no / is never a no"), the concluding statement, another negative assertion, calls attention to the tiger's real superiority ("you / know that it is not necessary to live in order to be alive").

"Melancthon" (1918) has a similar pattern of negative constructions: the elephant-speaker, in the opening statement, tells of its activities "which please / no one but myself," and later describes its skin "through which no light / can filter" (CP, 45–48). The negative statement is also used in the previously quoted climax of the poem:

> I see
> and I hear, unlike the
> wandlike body of which one hears so much,
> which was made
> to see and not to see; to hear and not to hear; . . .
>   (CP, 47)

We hear it again in the concluding rhetorical question: will, Melancthon asks, "depth be depth, thick skin be thick, to one who can see no / beautiful element of unreason under it?" (CP, 48).

These negative constructions provide meaningful concurrences, like the patterning of repetitions and assertions, illustrations and climactic statements. Moreover, the repetitions of "nothing," "no," "not" and "never" focus attention on the speaker's thought process because of the intricate sentence structures they encourage. In many of the poems there is a pattern of fluctuation between a progression of thought, expressed in the negative, and an illustration, given in the affirmative. In "To a Steam Roller," for example, a negative assertion ("The illustration / is nothing to you without the application") is contrasted with two affirmative statements that are illustrative amplifications of the steam roller's activities ("You crush all the particles down" and "Sparkling chips of rock / are crushed down"). There follows a negative statement that emphasizes the speaker's reflection:

Were not "impersonal judgment in aesthetic
    matters, a metaphysical impossibility," you

might fairly achieve
it.

(CPMM, 84)

During the transitional years (from 1919 through 1924), for the
devices that led to the internal arguments of the later work, the poet
transformed, rather than abandoned, the rhetorical figures that generated the earlier cadences. For example, "correction," that Renaissance method of amplifying a matter by comparing it with one that is
greater or smaller, is the principle underlying the poetry's patterns of
negative statements. When the animals of "Old Tiger" are described
as being "nothing to you," the device of correction amplifies the
tiger's apparent superiority that is contradicted in the course of the
argument. In the poems of the twenties, "correction" is replaced by
the device of "self-correction," which conveys a process of perception
rather than debate. When the speaker of "Silence" quotes her father
as saying, " 'The deepest feeling always shows itself in silence; / not
in silence, but restraint' " (CPMM, 91), the words "shows" and "not"
in these two lines, which close a long quotation, correspond to the
words "shown" and "never" in two lines that open the quotation:
" 'Superior people never make long visits, / have to be shown Longfellow's grave.' " The device has a patterning effect, for the concur-
rence of sound and meaning serves the versification of rhythm close
to prose.

Another of the poet's experiments in patterning poems of this
period is versifying prose quotations that contain figures of self-
correction, paradox, and other devices of apposition that characterize
poetic speech as well as poetic movement of thought. The incorpora-
tion of prose material, which Moore began in fall 1915, was associ-
ated with freedom from conventional meter, coinciding with the
beginning of free rhythm (as in "To Statecraft Embalmed") and
coexisting with the earliest devices of metaphysical argumentation.
By versifying prose as varied as Turgenev's *Fathers and Sons* and
statements by Dr. E. H. Kellogg of Carlisle's Presbyterian Church,
she unified poetry with the language of everyday life and yet preserved the tensions between them.

In poems of the early twenties, prose material is used to objectify the search for knowledge in a world of shifting definitions, a search that is futile from the outset. Nearly all of the quotations in "Marriage" (1923) contain words or phrases that are repeated in ways that reverse their meaning, as in paradox and self-correction. For example, Adam's conversation is about " 'past states, the present state, / seals, promises' " (CPMM, 64), we learn in a self-corrective quotation from Richard Baxter's *The Saints' Everlasting Rest*. In another paradoxical quotation from Baxter's book, Adam is said to be "impelled by 'the illusion of a fire / effectual to extinguish fire' " (CPMM, 65). Often the poet uses only the self-corrective in the quoted statement: when she presents Adam's strange fascination as "something feline, / something colubrine" (CPMM, 63), she employs only the conflicting element in Philip Littell's sentence, which reads in its entirety, "We were puzzled and we were fascinated, as if by something feline, something colubrine" (CPMM, 271). These constructions are set against similar ones in the poet's voice ("ivory white, snow white, / oyster white, and six others"; and "with its silence— / not its silence but its silences"—CPMM, 63, 64). The effect is an interplay of "voices" that suggest an actively moving consciousness, analogous to Pound's use of personae in Cantos I and II. The realization that marriage is "that striking grasp of opposites / opposed each to the other" (CPMM, 69) is a statement that describes a process of thought, and is reinforced rhythmically by the repeated use of figures of opposition.

Rhythmic effects of the later poetry are based on the struggle between alternating images that characterizes the creative process. Although ironic figures and negative constructions were used to emphasize rhythmic divisions of earlier poems, their use was in keeping with the poet's modern variation of metaphysical argumentation. In the later work the poet's use of irony captures the flow of thought. It is a principle of psychic law that irony and negativism characterize consciousness, for both are effects of representation through the opposite. Freud has written: "Dreams are not merely fond of representing two contraries by one and the same composite structure, but they . . . often change something in the dream-thoughts into its opposite. . . ."[14]

The observation is useful in considering the rhetoric of the later poems as well as the argumentative tensions that move them forward. Just as the two-part rhythmic division of an early version of "Sun" ("Fear is Hope," in *Observations* [1924]) is reinforced by contrasting negative and affirmative constructions at the beginnings of either stanza ("'No man'" and "Sun"—O, 15), the two-part rhythmic division of "No Swan So Fine" (1932) is emphasized by negative and affirmative openings to either part ("'No water so still'" and "Lodged in the Louis Fifteenth / candelabrum-tree"— CPMM, 19). In both cases the negative openings are quoted lines— the first by John Skelton, the second by Percy Phillip—that generate the poet's response to their rhythm and ideas. In the later composition, though, the poet uses a sentence fragment to indicate the diction of thought. And the response it initiates is less logical: in the earlier composition the poet disputes the opening idea; in the later one she links two opposite images (live swan, china swan) that the initial contrast reminds her of.

Another of the rhythmic devices patterning the later poems in accordance with the struggle of consciousness is the repetition of words in a series, unpunctuated and sometimes linked by "and." The refrains of "fighting fighting fighting" in "In Distrust of Merits" and of "marching marching marching" in "'Keeping Their World Large'" correspond to other three-stress phrases with falling rhythm, and the iterations characterize the poet as one who is painfully trying to understand. In "The Pangolin" corresponding recurrences of words are presented in three-stress phrases and set among longer phrases as a heightening device: they emphasize the poet's wonder at the discovery of those similar and opposite characteristics that man and anteater share. The poet, contemplating the pangolin, arrives at a new definition of man: "'Again the sun! / anew each day; and new and new and new'" (CPMM, 120). The three-stress phrase, which recurs in this poem, reinforces the poet's device of balancing two contrary images, perceiving the nature of one while contemplating the other.

Musical effects serve the discursive tone of early poems, such as "Old Tiger," in which open vowel sounds are heard in nearly all of the assertions, which are in the diction of direct address. Alliteration and assonance distinguish the amplifications, in the tone of formal discourse. These effects pattern the freer rhythms of the

poems from 1916 through 1919. In the later poetry sonic methods
enrich the "amplifications" of inner argumentation, or the poet's
ways of magnifying subjects in the diction of thought:

> The split
> pine fair hair, steady gannet-clear
> eyes and the pine-needled-path deer-
> swift step; that is Sweden, land of the
> free and the soil for a spruce-tree— . . .
>   (CPMM, 131–32)

In this passage from "A Carriage from Sweden" (1944) the poet
arrives at a definition of reality, the meaning of Sweden (like "that is
a mammal" in "The Pangolin" and "that is repose" in "Elephants")
by means of association rather than discursive logic. Supporting the
association are corresponding vowel sounds ("fair hair," "clear /
eyes" and "deer- / swift"), and rhymes, as well as off-rhymes, at both
ends of last lines of stanzas ("free" and "tree," above), that capture
the sensation of the carriage in motion.

The musical pattern of "The Steeple-Jack," "The Student," and
"The Hero" sustains the structural unity of what I believe to be a
remarkable sequence, despite the fact that the three poems have not
appeared collectively since their first magazine publication in *Poetry*
(1932).[15] The three titular images named in "The Steeple-Jack"—
"The Hero, the student, / the steeple-jack"—are figures of perception, constituting insight and reverence for mystery; all promise
"hope," that quality defined in "The Hero" as arriving when "all
ground for hope has vanished" (CPMM, 9). The sequence is bound
together by recurrent overlapping words such as "danger," "hope,"
"hero," "see." In "The Steeple-Jack" the word "see" recurs and is
echoed by puns ("sea" and "C. J. Poole," his name), and in "The
Student" the *ee* and *o* sounds are subdued, but exist. In "The Hero"
the *o* sounds provide the tapestry of end rhymes linking the first, last
and penultimate lines of each stanza; in addition, the *ee* and *o* notes
throughout the poem echo its key words, "hero" and "see." "The
Hero" concludes with a restatement of the relation of heroism to
perception:

> He's not out
> seeing a sight but the rock

crystal thing to see—the startling El Greco
  brimming with inner light—that
covets nothing that it has let go. This then you may know
as the hero.

(CPMM, 9)

Largely because of the sonic design, which assists the poet's association of "hero" and "seer" or "student," we find that the three figures are a composite image of the effort to see clearly. This struggle, dramatized in "The Mind Is an Enchanting Thing," is the basis of the later poetics.

"The Mind Is an Enchanting Thing" typifies the poem that is structured in several parts, at least two of them corresponding, and in which rhythmic divisions are based on shifts in tone. This poem has four sections, the first and fourth having rhythmic resemblances. According to a method of scansion based on the conversational phrase, each rhetorical group is measured by the number of phrases within it and characterized by the stress patterns of the phrases.[16] The natural phrase (which the poet has said is the vocal unit of her poetry) tells us how the poem is to be spoken, or read with an ear for speaking it aloud. Correspondences are determined by the audible duration of rhetorical levels in the poem's structure. Of course, although the duration of shifts is audible, the precise numbers of phrases within them is not. Nevertheless, the existence of rhythmic divisions that correspond numerically and are based on shifts in tone tells us that the pattern exists in the poem. Further, it is found in abundance in the poetry of Marianne Moore.

THE MÍND IS AN ENCHÁNTING THING
is an enchánted thíng |
    like the gláze on a
kátydid-wíng |
        subdivíded by sún
            till the néttings are légion. |
Like Gíeseking pláying Scarlátti; |

    like the ápteryx-áwl
        as a béak, | or the

kiwi's rain-shawl
      of haired feathers, | the mind
      feeling its way as though blind, |
walks along with its eyes on the ground. |

It has memory's ear
      that can hear without
having to hear. |
      Like the gyroscope's fall,
      truly unequivocal |
because trued by regnant certainty, |

it is a power of
      strong enchantment. | It
is like the dove-
      neck animated by
      sun; | it is memory's eye;
it's conscientious inconsistency. |

It tears off the veil; | tears
    the temptation, | the
mist the heart wears, |
      from its eyes— | if the heart
      has a face; | it takes apart
dejection. | It's fire in the dove-neck's

iridescence; | in the
    inconsistencies
of Scarlatti. |
      Unconfusion submits
      its confusion to proof; | it's
not a Herod's oath that cannot change. |

The numerical pattern of the audible argumentative shifts are charted as follows, in terms of the rhetorical device that characterizes a section, the number of conversational phrases within it and the number of stresses per phrase:

I. First two stanzas:
  a. Self-corrective assertion and amplification, four phrases, 4-3-4-3.
  b. Amplification and new assertion, four phrases, 3-4-4-4.

II. Stanzas three and four:
  a. Paradox, three phrases, 5-4-3.
  b. Amplification and new assertion, three phrases, 3-4-4.

III. Stanza five, climax, eight short phrases, 2-2-3-1-2-3-3.

IV. Conclusion, four phrases, 4-3-5-5.

Each section contains one or more rhetorical devices that contribute to the "inner dialectic" that moves the poem forward to illumination. The first assertion is self-corrective, indicating the diction of thought ("The Mind Is an Enchanting Thing / is an enchanted thing"). The first simile, of the sun-glazed "katydid-wing," amplifies the first assertion; the second, of "Gieseking playing Scarlatti," is a magnifying amplification of the second assertion ("feeling its way as though blind, / walks along with its eyes on the ground"). The phrase "as though blind" recalls the "objection foreseen" of the earlier poetry; here it is used ironically, fulfilling the requirement of dialectic, that the contrary of a position, later refuted (by "it is memory's eye"), is stated with vividness.

The second section (stanzas three and four) begins with a shift to paradox, and the phrase length contracts sharply. The paradox ("that can hear without / having to hear"), indicating another level of the diction of thought, is at variance with "feeling its way as though blind," in that perception takes place without the perceiving sense. The next assertion ("it is a power of / strong enchantment") is amplified by the image of the gyroscope whose fall from gravity is "truly unequivocal / because trued by regnant certainty." The mind's "enchantment," or power of transformation, is in its capacity to illuminate a problem by "falling" and correcting itself.

The climax has the greatest rhythmic variation, consisting of six short phrases. The poet displays the mind's struggle toward illumination in self-corrective figures ("it tears off the veil; tears / the temptation" and "from its eyes—if the heart / has a face"). The mind, analyzing a situation, reaches the feelings, prepared for by the vivid evocations of memory. And the self-corrective figures illustrate the mind's pivotal power, like the gyroscope's remarkable turning.

The last section returns to the rhythm of section one. Here, images used before the climax as similes ("Scarlatti," "dove-neck") are given as metaphors, following the change of "sun" to "fire." The dialectic properties of fire are implicitly attributed to the mind, for it is in the mind's capacity to change that perception is gained. In this poem the rhythmic divisions correspond to paradoxes and self-corrections that enable us to hear the inner drama of illumination. In "Critics and Connoisseurs," an earlier poem, whose rhythmic divisions correspond with rhetorical shifts in the scheme of metaphysical argumentation, what we hear is the person arguing against unenlightened striving ("I have seen ambition without / understanding"); in the later one we hear the flow of thought. Although both debates concern blindness and vision, the conflict of the later poem is heard in inner shifts that are conjoined with the imagery of perceptual change.

Obviously, numbers serve only to show the pattern of what is actually heard in a poem, whether they are used to measure syllables, antithetical images, balanced statements, or my system of corresponding conversational stresses. Essentially, though, I believe that Marianne Moore has made great poetry out of prose rhythms by using techniques that formalize them, insuring the naturalness of her verse. From her earliest experiments in free verse, she structured her poems on the disciplines of argumentation, from the discursive strategies of the formative work to the "inner dialectic" structures of the later poetry. These techniques are the basis for her poetry as a spoken art.

VI

The Passion
for Real Things

From the beginning the poetry of Marianne Moore has been built on her excitement for real things and, as she said of Henry James, "the rapture of observation" (P, 29). The proper study of her art, then, is in her techniques of transforming and the effects of transmuting those photographs, illustrations, facts, quotations, museum tapestries, guidebooks and exhibits that captured her imagination.

In a letter of 1925 Marianne Moore wrote: "Notes appended to my book [*Observations*] will show that reading and the conversations of my friends have been the inspiration of my work." In the letter to P. Casper Harvey of the Missouri Writers' Guild, who had requested information about her work, she cited Chaucer, Spenser, and Defoe, as well as "Tilden's books on tennis and articles in the Journal of Natural History."[1]

Laurence Stapleton illuminates the poet's transmutation of material when she writes: "The poems—the composition—are the "proofs" Marianne Moore had to find for things she had known for years." She compares Marianne Moore's intuitive method to that of Sir Isaac Newton, who would, in brief periods, find "proofs" for what he had known instinctively to be true.[2]

Another important insight into her working methods is in an editorial comment of a 1979 *Marianne Moore Newsletter*. Throughout her work, Patricia C. Willis observes, Marianne Moore has used three kinds of evidence: the first is direct personal observation, although we know that when the poet writes "I saw" an object or animal, the experience might have been with a picture of it in a magazine; the second is a quotation, from a friend, her brother, a teacher, or a passerby; the third is from a book she has read, and is often found among her notebook entries, if not actually given in her notes to the poems.[3] That is the importance of the archival collection in understanding the workings of her imagination on her material.

In the same article Marianne Moore is quoted as having said, in a radio broadcast of 1951:

> Books, conversation, a remark, objects, circumstances, sometimes make an indelible impression on one, and a few words which occurred to one at the time the impression was made, remain associated with the original impression and suggest other words. Then, upon scrutiny, these words seem to have distorted the concept, so the effort to effect a record of what seemed valuable—say a testimony to the impression made, is abandoned perhaps, but remains dormant. Then perhaps the original impression reasserts itself with added associative detail and results in a suitable development. For instance, you see a suit of armor. The moveability suggests a wearer—there's life under the mechanism; you are reminded of an armadillo, say, or a crayfish, and recall the beauty of the ancient testudo, the shield laid on the shield of the Romans. Then perhaps the idea of conflict counteracts that of romance. Presently you see a live iguana and are startled by the paradox of its docility in connection with its horrific aspect. The idea of beauty outweighs the thought of painful self-protectiveness, and you have a developing theme.[4]

The poet's remarks help us to see not only how she transforms the object, but also how the mind, focusing on the object, leads to associations that call forth fresh conclusions about bravery, or freedom, or beauty.

We have seen that process at work in many of the poems. The background of "No Swan So Fine," for example, is that the poet, saddened by the death of Lord Balfour in 1930, observed a china swan on one of a pair of Louis XV candelabra which had belonged to the late statesman. Actually, she had "seen" the candelabrum pictured in a Christie's sale announcement in the *Illustrated London*

News (28 June 1930, p. 1211), and had sketched it in her notebook. In May 1931 the poet read, as it has been recounted, an article on the restoration of Versailles in the *New York Times Magazine*. In the article she found a sentence, "There is no water so still as the dead fountains of Versailles," and wrote it above a photograph of a still fountain in her copy of the magazine.

From these quotations and from the "observation" of the china swan, sketched in her notebook, the poet wrote of the passing of beauty, as well as its permanence:[5]

> Lodged in the Louis Fifteenth
>   candelabrum-tree of cockscomb-
> tinted buttons, dahlias,
> sea-urchins, and everlastings,
>   it perches on the branching foam
> of polished sculptured
> flowers—at ease and tall. The king is dead.
>   (CPMM, 19)

In like manner, "Four Quartz Crystal Clocks" contains the poet's observation and notes, which lead to the central idea. The poem begins with precise, factual information:

> There are four vibrators, the world's exactest clocks;
>   and these quartz time-pieces that tell
> time intervals to other clocks,
>   these worksless clocks work well;
> independently the same, kept in
>   the 41° Bell
>   Laboratory time
>
> vault.
>   (CPMM, 115)

Setting a standard for accuracy, the poet meditates on a world of fallacy, inexactness, and imprecision. Her "observation" in this poem was based on a flyer from one of her telephone bills which described "The World's Most Accurate 'Clocks'" at the Bell Telephone Laboratories.[6] The "observation" led to references from her

reading, all given in her notes to the poem: Jean Giraudoux's statement, in *Figaro*, that some Arabs are ignorant of Napoleon's death,
and references to Chronos and Jupiter from Brewer's *Dictionary of
Phrase and Fable*. Thus her meditation on the ideal of precision and
its distortion in the world. In this way the mind, concentrating on
an object or a vividly imagined scene, moves forward to an understanding, making us aware of ideas mirrored in common things.

In poems of the early twenties, prose material is used to objectify
the quest for an awareness of modern life that, ironically, cannot be
found. The speaker of "People's Surroundings" (1922), examining a
modern metropolis, considers a list of facts only to declare, "these are
questions more than answers" (CPMM, 56). The mountain of "An
Octopus" (1924) changes metamorphically as the eye moves over it
despite the ordering quotations from the *National Parks Portfolio*. In
"Marriage" the inquiring speaker helplessly exclaims, "Psychology
which explains everything / explains nothing" (CPMM, 62).

Her poetics is built on an aesthetic of inquiry, the artistic process
of asking why. The search for answers is life's major concern, and
one which is nearly always thwarted. That quest creates the tension
between the world and the object on which the mind dwells and,
although a solution is never found, there is usually a leap forward
from darkness to sight.

In my study of the poet's engagement with the world, I have not
examined her concerns with topical matters. However, the development of her aesthetic of inquiry does happen to coincide with her
preoccupation with events of the century. Although she had been,
from girlhood, engaged with the world around her, she became
profoundly involved with political matters in her middle and later
years. In an address to the Grolier Club in 1948 she intimated her
sense of a vital connection between poetry and politics: "In times
like these we are tempted to disregard anything that has not a direct
bearing on freedom; or should I say, an obvious bearing, for what is
more persuasive than poetry. . . ." (P, 12).

Fifteen years later, in the Voice of America broadcast, she was to
put the matter more directly. Asked whether her work had changed
"in character or style" since she began writing, she replied: "I am
today much aware of the world's dilemma. People's effect on other
people results, it seems to me, in an enforced sense of respon-
sibility—a compulsory obligation to participate in others' prob-

lems."[7] An essay in the *Nation*, "We Will Walk Like the Tapir," contains a strong criticism of human indifference. It begins: " 'Savage' and 'brutal' are false terms, the brute is so often the man."[8]

Nevertheless, her best effects are in poems that may have been inspired by public events, but transcend them by encompassing larger ideas, such as the passage in "He 'Digesteth Harde Yron'" (1941):

> The power of the visible
> is the invisible; as even where
> no tree of freedom grows,
> so-called brute courage knows.
>   (CPMM, 100)

In fact, creativity, for Marianne Moore, rises from the subtle dialectic between freedom and repression. We learn of this struggle for freedom from the camel-sparrow that survives in "He 'Digesteth Harde Yron,'" from the figure of Hercules, who "was hindered to succeed" in "The Paper Nautilus," from the salamander in "His Shield" who knows that freedom is "the power of relinquishing / what one would keep" (CPMM, 99, 121, 144).

In her poetry freedom is built on the very limitations that life imposes. Just as the poet's fascination with worldly things is generated by life's boundaries, her concept of freedom is that liberty which is won despite the laws of restraint. In "Idiosyncracy and Technique" (1956) she wrote of the artistic process: "Creative secrets, are they secrets? Impassioned interest in life, that burns its bridges behind it and will not contemplate defeat, is one, I would say" (MMR, 181).

And her meditative poem, "What Are Years," deals with a restricted freedom that is, paradoxically, the source of all creative energy. Its aesthetic is, I believe, at the basis of the poetry of Marianne Moore. Indeed, it is her faith:

>   He
> sees deep and is glad, who
>   accedes to mortality
> and in his imprisonment rises
> upon himself as

the sea in a chasm, struggling to be
free and unable to be,
  in its surrendering
  finds its continuing.

So he who strongly feels,
behaves. The very bird,
  grown taller as he sings, steels
his form straight up. Though he is captive,
his mighty singing
says, satisfaction is a lowly
thing, how pure a thing is joy.
  This is mortality,
  this is eternity.

(CPMM, 95)

Notes

Introduction

1. Margaret Anderson, in a note appended to Marianne Moore's "You Say You Said," *Little Review* 4 (1918), 56–58; rpt. in *The Little Review Anthology* (New York: Hermitage House, 1953), pp. 187–88.

2. Harriet Monroe, *Poetry* 19 (1922), 208–16.

3. Ezra Pound, *The Letters of Ezra Pound* 1907–1941, ed. D. D. Paige (New York: Harcourt, Brace, 1950), p. 144.

4. T. S. Eliot, "Marianne Moore," *Dial* 75 (1923); rpt. in Charles Tomlinson, ed., *Marianne Moore: A Collection of Critical Essays*, Twentieth Century Views (Englewood Cliffs, N. J.: Prentice Hall, 1969), p. 48.

5. Hilda Doolittle [H. D.], "Marianne Moore," *Egoist* 3 (1916), 118–19.

6. Tomlinson, p. 49.

7. William Carlos Williams, "Marianne Moore," *Dial* 78 (1925), 401; rpt. in Tomlinson, p. 59.

8. R. P. Blackmur, "The Method of Marianne Moore," in *The Double Agent: Essays in Craft and Elucidation* (New York: Arrow Editions, 1935); rpt. in Tomlinson, pp. 66–86.

9. "Marianne Moore Issue," *Quarterly Review of Literature* 4 (1948); Stevens, 143–49; Williams, 126; Frankenberg, 192.

10. Randall Jarrell, "The Country Was," *Partisan Review* 9 (1942), 58–60.

11. Randall Jarrell, "The Humble Animal," *Kenyon Review* 4 (1942); "His Shield" (1953), both in *Poetry and the Age* (New York: Vintage-Knopf, 1953; Ecco, 1980), pp. 162–66.

12. Pound, *Letters*, p. 143.

I. New York: Marianne Moore as a Characteristic American

1. Pound, *Letters*, p. 144. All quotations from Ezra Pound in this chapter are from this letter (pp. 141–44) and are cited in text.

2. Marianne Moore, "A Letter to Ezra Pound," in Tomlinson, p. 17. Quotations from the 1919 letter are from this edition, pp. 16–20, and hereafter will be cited in text.

3. An earlier version of "Dock Rats" in *Poems* (London: Egoist Press, 1921) reads, "all palms and tail."

4. Marianne Moore, "English Literature Since 1914," in *Marianne Moore Newsletter* 4, no. 2 (Fall 1980), 13–21.

5. The letter was written in answer to Harvey's request for information about her work for the *Kansas City Journal-Post*. See *Marianne Moore Newsletter* 4, no. 1 (Spring 1980), 15.

6. "Marianne Moore," *Current Biography* 24 (1968), 27.

7. [Unsigned comment], *Marianne Moore Newsletter* 5, no. 1 (Spring 1981), 3.

8. Donald Hall, ed., "The Art of Poetry IV: Marianne Moore," *Paris Review* 26 (1961), 45.

9. Originally published in *Hound & Horn* 7 (1934), 372.

10. Letter to Dorothea Gray, 5 November 1935, *Marianne Moore Newsletter* 2, no. 2 (Fall 1978), 9.

11. Originally published in *Vogue*, 1 August 1960.

12. Walt Whitman, *Leaves of Grass: Comprehensive Readers Edition*, ed. Harold W. Blodgett and Sculley Bradley (New York: Norton, 1965), pp. 160–61.

13. Marianne Moore, "American Poetry," Forum Lectures, Voice of America, 7 December 1963, p. 2; notes to "The Student," *CPMM*, p. 278. Lisa Steinman makes the connection between Moore and Emerson in "Moore, Emerson and Kreymborg: The Use of Lists in 'The Monkeys,'" *Marianne Moore Newsletter* 4, no. 1 (Spring 1980), 7–10; Laurence Stapleton, *Marianne Moore: The Poet's Advance* (Princeton, N. J.: Princeton University Press, 1978), also writes of Marianne Moore's affinity with Emerson (p. 58).

14. Among many references to visual perception in Emerson's writings are "The eye is the first circle," in "Circles" (p. 212); and "This insight, which expresses itself by what is called Imagination, is a very high sort of seeing, which does not come by study, but by the intellect being where and what it sees, by sharing the path, or circuit of things through forms, and so making them translucid to others." See Ralph Waldo Emerson, "The Poet," in *Essays* (New York: Crowell, 1926; New York: Harper & Row, 1951), pp. 278–79.

15. Ezra Pound, *Patria Mia* (Chicago: R. F. Seymour, 1950), p. 74.

16. Letter to Pound is in the Rosenbach Museum and Library.

17. Moore, "American Poetry," p. 1.

18. *Omaggio a Marianne Moore*, Comp. Vanni Scheiwiller (Milan: All'insegna del Pesce d'Oro, 1964), ltd. 1000 copies; rpt. in Grace Schulman, "Notes on the Development of 'Old Tiger' by Marianne Moore," in *Antaeus* 30–31 (Summer–Autumn 1978), 34–40.

19. Originally published in *Sewanee Review* 52 (1944), 500.

20. Originally published in *Poetry* 21 (1931), 35.

21. Moore, "American Poetry," p. 2.

22. Although "What Are Years" has a question mark in *CPMM*, the punctuation is omitted in references to the poem throughout this study because of Marianne Moore's stated objection to it. Grace Schulman, "A Conversation with Marianne Moore," *Quarterly Review of Literature* 16, nos. 1–2 (1969), 164.

II. A Way of Seeing: The Poetics of Inquiry

1. Rosenbach 1251. Rosenbach Museum and Library.

2. Rosenbach 1251. Rosenbach Museum and Library.

3. Moore, "American Poetry," p. 2.

4. *Oeuvres de Rimbaud*, ed. Suzanne Bernard (Classiques Garnier, 1960), p. 346.

5. Charles Baudelaire, *Les Fleurs du Mal*, ed. J. Crépet and G. Blin (Paris: José Corti, 1942), pp. 9–10.

6. Hall, "The Art of Poetry," p. 51.

7. Schulman, "A Conversation with Marianne Moore," p. 163.

8. William Carlos Williams, *Paterson* (1946–58; reprint, New York: New Directions, 1963), p. 248.

9. La Fontaine, *Fables Choisies* (1693–94), ed. Beverly S. Ridgely (New Brunswick, N. J.: Rutgers University Press, 1967), pp. 36–38.

10. Williams, *Paterson*, p. 14.

III. The Evolution of an Inner Dialectic from Argumentation to Reverie

1. Marianne Moore, "Sun!," *Contemporary Verse* 1 (1916), 7. The final version, the seventh of its published variants, appears in *CPMM*, p. 234.

2. "Progress," *Tipyn O'Bob* 4 (1909), 10.

3. Schulman, "A Conversation with Marianne Moore," p. 158.

4. Originally published as "To the Soul of 'Progress,'" *Egoist* 2 (1915), 62.

5. Sir Herbert Grierson, Introduction to *Metaphysical Lyrics and Poems of the Seventeenth Century* (Oxford: Clarendon Press, 1921), p. xxxiv.

6. Louis Martz, *The Poetry of Meditation: A Study in English Religious Literature of the Seventeenth Century* (New Haven, Conn.: Yale University Press, 1954), p. 39.

7. "MM's Reading in English Literature, 1905–1907," *Marianne Moore Newsletter* 5, no. 1 (Spring 1981), 15.

8. Rosamund Tuve writes that diminution is "an orthodox variant of amplifying." She explains that "figures under amplification are not used to expatiate; they are used to magnify, to make more impressive, more worthy of attention" (*Elizabethan and Metaphysical Imagery: Renaissance Poetic and Twentieth-Century Critics* [Chicago: University of Chicago Press, 1947], p. 90).

9. Tomlinson, p. 49.

10. *Others* 2 (1916), 5.

11. Tuve, p. 206.

12. G. H. Mair, ed., *Wilson's Arte of Rhetorique* (1560) (Oxford: Clarendon, 1909), p. 186.

13. M. L. Rosenthal has written about self-correction in Marianne Moore's poetry in *The Modern Poets: A Critical Introduction* (New York: Oxford, 1965), pp. 140–48.

14. Quoted in Martz, p. 27.

15. D. H. Lawrence, *Etruscan Places* (London: Martin Secker, 1932), p. 97; *The Collected Poems of Wallace Stevens* (New York: Knopf, 1954), p. 320.

16. Letter to Barbara Kurz, *Marianne Moore Newsletter* 1, no. 2 (Fall 1977), 7.

17. Letter to Barbara Kurz, p. 7.

18. Informal conversation with the author.

19. "No Swan So Fine," *Marianne Moore Newsletter* 2, no. 2 (Spring 1978), 3.

20. Paul Valéry, *Selected Writings*, tr. Thomas McGreevy, Anthony Bower, et al. (New York: New Directions), p. 99.

21. Sigmund Freud, *The Standard Edition of the Complete Psychological Works of Sigmund Freud*, tr. James Strachey et al., ed. James Strachey, vol. 5, (London: Hogarth Press, 1953–66), p. 596. All subsequent citations are from this edition and will be referred to as *Standard Edition*.

22. Freud, *Standard Edition*, vol. 4, p. 318.

23. See Martz, pp. 67, 68, 278, 321, and elsewhere.

IV. The Mind's Transforming Power: Metamorphic Imagery and the Poetry of Engagement

1. The drafts resided in the Rosenbach archives for years, and were finally assembled, according to the author's intentions, in the *Yale Review* 74 (1985), 700–706.

2. From the typescript of "Radical" in the Rosenbach Museum & Library.

3. Letter in the Rosenbach Museum & Library.

4. Ezra Pound, *The Cantos of Ezra Pound* (Norfolk, Conn.: New Directions, 1970), p. 17.

5. Reprinted as part of "A Retrospect" in *Literary Essays of Ezra Pound*, ed. T. S. Eliot (Norfolk, Conn.: New Directions, 1954), p. 4.

6. Marianne Moore, "You Are Like the Realistic Product of an Idealistic Search for Gold at the Foot of the Rainbow" ("To a Chameleon"), *Egoist* 3 (1916), 71.

7. "Sun!" in *Contemporary Verse* 1 (1916), 7; "Fear Is Hope" in *Observations*; as "Sun" in *The Mentor Book of Religious Verse*, ed. Horace Gregory and Marya Zaturenska (New York: New American Library, 1957); as "'Sun'" in *A Marianne Moore Reader* and *The Arctic Ox*; as "Sun" in *Tell Me, Tell Me* and *The Complete Poems*.

8. See Freud's comments on "Condensation" or the combination of opposites in dream in *Standard Edition*, vol. 4, p. 174.

V. "A Quite New Rhythm": The Spoken Art of Marianne Moore's Poetry

1. Tomlinson, p. 49.

2. See, for example, Blackmur and Jarrell, in Tomlinson, pp. 66–86 and pp. 162–66; also W. H. Auden, *The Dyer's Hand and Other Essays* (New York: Random House, 1962), pp. 296–97.

3. Tomlinson, p. 9.

4. Stapleton, p. 215. Quoted from a note she provided for the *Oxford Anthology of American Literature*, ed. William Rose Benét and Norman Holmes Pearson (New York, 1941), p. 1319.

5. Letter to Thomas P. Murphy in *Marianne Moore Newsletter* 5, no. 2 (Fall 1981), 15.

6. Hall, "The Art of Poetry," p. 54.

7. Schulman, "A Conversation with Marianne Moore," p. 162.

8. Marianne Moore, "The Accented Syllable," *Egoist* 3 (1916), 151–52.

9. Schulman, "A Conversation with Marianne Moore," p. 162.

10. "When I Buy Pictures," *Dial* 71 (1921), 33.

11. Benjamin Hrushovsky, "On Free Rhythms in Modern Poetry," in *Style in Language*, ed. T. A. Sebeok (Cambridge, Mass.: Technology Press of Massachusetts Institute of Technology, 1960), p. 185.

12. "That Harp You Play So Well," *Poetry* 4 (1915), 70.

13. "The Past Is the Present" (untitled), in *Others* 1 (1915), 106.

14. Sigmund Freud, *Standard Edition*, vol. 3, p. 174.

15. "Part of a Novel, Part of a Poem, Part of a Play," *Poetry* 40 (1951) 3, 119. "The Steeple-Jack" appears in *Selected Poems, Collected Poems, A Marianne Moore Reader*, and *Complete Poems;* "The Student," in *What Are Years* (revised) and in *Complete Poems;* "The Hero," in *Collected Poems* and *Complete Poems*.

16. The "scansion" of poems by groups rather than feet has appealed to a number of critics. Roger Mitchell, for example, has analyzed Whitman's structures on the basis of speech stresses in a two-part line ("A Prosody for Whitman?" *PMLA* 84 [1969], 1606–12). Sister M. Martin Barry has scanned Eliot's poems by lengths of groups in *An Analysis of the Prosodic Structure of Selected Poems of T. S. Eliot* (Washington, D. C.: Catholic University of America Press, 1948).

VI. The Passion for Real Things

1. Letter in Rosenbach collection, and printed in *Marianne Moore Newsletter* 4, no. 1 (Spring 1980), 15–16.

2. Stapleton, p. 156.

3. [Patricia C. Willis], "Comment," *Marianne Moore Newsletter* 3, no. 2 (Fall 1979), 2–4.

4. Willis, p. 2.

5. "'No Swan So Fine,'" *Marianne Moore Newsletter* 2, no. 2 (Spring 1978), 2–5. All material is in the Rosenbach collection. See Marianne Moore's Reading Diary, 1930–43 (1250/6).

6. "'Four Quartz Crystal Clocks,'" *Marianne Moore Newsletter* 5, no. 2 (Fall 1981), 15–16.

7. "American Poetry," p. 1.

8. "We Shall Walk Like the Tapir," *Nation*, 25 June 1943, 866–67.

Bibliography

WORKS BY MARIANNE MOORE

Moore, Marianne. "American Poetry." Forum Lectures, Voice of America. 7 December 1963. *The Arctic Ox.* London: Faber and Faber, 1964.

———. *Collected Poems.* New York: Macmillan, 1951.

———. *Complete Poems.* New York: Macmillan and Viking, 1967; London: Faber and Faber, 1968; New York: Viking, 1981.

———. *Eight Poems Written by Marianne Moore, with Drawings by Robert Andrew Parker, Hand-Colored by the Artist.* New York: The Museum of Modern Art, 1962. Ltd. 195 copies.

———. *The Fables of La Fontaine.* London: Faber and Faber, 1954.

———. *Like a Bulwark.* New York: Viking, 1956.

———. *A Marianne Moore Reader.* New York: Viking, 1959.

———. *Marianne Moore Reading Her Own Poems.* Harvard Vocarium Records P-1064, 1944.

———. *Marianne Moore Reading Her Poems and Fables from La Fontaine.* Caedmon TC 1025, 1955.

———. *Nevertheless.* New York: Macmillan, 1944.

———. *Omaggio a Marianne Moore.* Comp. Vanni Scheiwiller. Milan: All' insegna del Pesce d'Oro, 1964. Ltd. 1000 copies.

———. *O to Be a Dragon.* New York: Viking, 1959.

———. *The Pangolin and Other Verse.* London: Brendin, 1936.

———. *Poems.* London: Egoist Press, 1921.

———. *Predilections.* New York: Viking, 1955.

———, tr. *Puss in Boots, the Sleeping Beauty and Cinderella: A Retelling of Three Classic Fairy Tales Based on the French of Charles Perrault.* New York: Macmillan, 1963.

———. *Selected Poems.* New York: Macmillan, 1935.

———. "Selections from a Poet's Reading Diary and Sketchbooks." *Tiger's Eye* 1 (1947), 20–35. Reprint. New York: Kraus Reprint Editions, 1967.

——. *Tell Me, Tell Me: Granite, Steel, and Other Topics.* New York: Viking and Macmillan, 1967.

——. *Unfinished Poems by Marianne Moore.* Philadelphia: Philip H. and A. S. W. Rosenbach Foundation, 1972.

——. *What Are Years.* New York: Macmillan, 1941.

BIBLIOGRAPHIES

Abbot, Craig S. *Marianne Moore: A Descriptive Bibliography.* Pittsburgh: University of Pittsburgh Press, 1977.

Sheehy, Eugene P., and K. A. Lohf, comps. *The Achievement of Marianne Moore: A Bibliography 1907–1957.* New York: New York Public Library, 1958.

RELEVANT WORKS

Anderson, Margaret, ed. *Little Review Anthology.* New York: Hermitage House, 1953.

Auden, W. H. *The Dyer's Hand and Other Essays.* New York: Random House, 1962.

Blackmur, R. P. *The Double Agent: Essays in Craft and Elucidation.* New York: Arrow Editions, 1935.

Bogan, Louise. *Achievement in American Poetry, 1900–1957.* Chicago: Henry Regnery, 1951.

Burke, Kenneth. "Motives and Motifs in the Poetry of Marianne Moore." *Accent* 2 (1942), 157–59.

Borroff, Marie. *Language and the Poet: Verbal Artistry in Frost, Stevens, and Moore.* Chicago: University of Chicago Press, 1979.

Costello, Bonnie. *Marianne Moore: Imaginary Possessions.* Cambridge, Mass.: Harvard University Press, 1981.

Engel, Bernard F. *Marianne Moore.* New York: Twayne, 1964.

Frankenberg, Lloyd. *Pleasure Dome.* Boston: Houghton-Mifflin, 1949.

Freud, Sigmund. *The Standard Edition of the Complete Psychological Works of Sigmund Freud.* Tr. James Strachey et al., ed. James Strachey. 24 vols. London: Hogarth Press, 1953–66.

Garrigue, Jean. *Marianne Moore.* University of Minnesota Pamphlets on American Writers, no. 50. Minneapolis: University of Minnesota Press, 1965.

Hall, Donald. *Marianne Moore: The Cage and the Animal.* Pegasus American Authors. New York: Western Publishing, 1970.

——, ed. "The Art of Poetry IV: Marianne Moore." *Paris Review* 26 (1961), 40–66.

Hollander, John. *Vision and Resonance.* New York: Oxford University Press, 1975.

Jarrell, Randall. "Two Essays on Marianne Moore: The Humble Animal; Her Shield." *Poetry and the Age.* New York: Vintage-Knopf, 1953; Ecco, 1980.

"Marianne Moore Issue." *Quarterly Review of Literature* 4 (1948). Essays by William Carlos Williams, Elizabeth Bishop, John Crowe Ransom, Wallace Stevens, Louis Bogan, Vivienne Koch, John L. Sweeney, Wallace Fowlie, Cleanth Brooks, Lloyd Frankenberg, T. C. Wilson, and George Dillon.

Martz, Louis L., *The Poetry of Meditation: A Study in English Religious Literature of the Seventeenth-Century.* New Haven, Conn.: Yale University Press, 1954.

Pearce, Roy Harvey. *The Continuity of American Poetry.* Princeton, N. J.: Princeton University Press, 1961.

Pound, Ezra. *Patria Mia.* Chicago: Ralph F. Seymour, 1950.

———. *The Letters of Ezra Pound, 1907–1941.* Ed. D. D. Paige. New York: Harcourt, Brace, 1950.

———. *Literary Essays of Ezra Pound.* Ed. T. S. Eliot. Norfolk, Conn.: New Directions, 1954.

Rosenthal, M. L. *The Modern Poets: A Critical Introduction.* New York: Oxford, 1965.

Schulman, Grace. "Conversation with Marianne Moore." *Quarterly Review of Literature* 16 (1969), 154–71.

Stapleton, Laurence. *Marianne Moore: The Poet's Advance.* Princeton, N. J.: Princeton University Press, 1978.

Tomlinson, Charles, ed. *Marianne Moore: A Collection of Critical Essays.* Twentieth Century Views. Englewood Cliffs, N. J.: Prentice-Hall, 1969, pp. 1–19.

Tuve, Rosamund. *Elizabethan and Metaphysical Imagery: Renaissance and Twentieth-Century Critics.* Chicago: University of Chicago Press, 1947.

Vendler, Helen. *Part of Nature, Part of Us: Modern American Poets.* Cambridge, Mass.: Harvard University Press, 1980.

Willis, Patricia, ed. *Marianne Moore Newsletter.* Spring 1977–Fall 1981. Philadelphia: Philip H. and A. S. W. Rosenbach Foundation.

Index

Aesop, 35–36
Acervate style, 14
Anderson, Margaret, 2
Atlantic Monthly, 17

Bacon, Francis, 11
Barry, Sister M. Martin, 127
Baudelaire, Charles, 28–29, 33–35, 37, 87
Baxter, Richard, 48, 58, 110
Bishop, Elizabeth, 4
Blackmur, R. P., 3–4, 127
Blake, William, 11, 24
Bogan, Louise, 4
Borroff, Marie, 5
Brooks, Cleanth, 3
Browne, Sir Thomas, 11
Bryn Mawr, 10, 11, 12, 48, 80
Bunyan, John, 11
Burke, Kenneth, 3, 4

Chaucer, Geoffrey, 35, 36, 117
Cicero, 14, 56
Conrad, Joseph, 11
Contradiction, the mind's growth by, 57, 62, 69, 70–76
Costello, Bonnie, 5
Craig, Gordon, 11
Cummings, E. E., 16

Defoe, Daniel, 11, 117
Dial, The, 3, 5, 99, 100
Donne, John, 48, 49, 51, 54, 55, 93
Dream, 69–70, 91–93

Egoist, The, 3, 12, 17, 47
Eliot, T. S., 2–3, 11, 12–13, 22, 28, 30–31, 34, 38, 39, 47–48, 49–50, 55, 97, 127
Emerson, Ralph Waldo, 13, 15, 124
Epanilepsis, 15

Fable tradition, 35–36, 41
Frankenberg, Lloyd, 4
French Symbolists, 22, 33–35, 41
Freud, Sigmund, 69–70, 91–92, 110–11, 127

Ghil, René, 10, 16
Gibbons, Richard, 58
Giraudoux, Jean, 120
Gray, Dorothea, 13
Grierson, Sir Herbert, 48, 97
Grosz, George, 24

Hall, Donald, 12, 34, 99
Hardy, Thomas, 11
Harvey, Caspar, 11
H. D. [Hilda Doolittle], 3, 11, 12
Herbert, George, 48, 49, 51, 54
Hopkins, Gerard Manley, 75

Horace, 35
Hrushovsky, Benjamin, 101
Hunt, Leigh, 11
Hyphenated words at line breaks, 17

Illustrated London News, 28
Inner dialectic, 43–75, 110–16

James, Henry, 11, 13, 15, 27, 28, 29, 117
Jammes, Francis, 34
Jarrell, Randall, 4–5, 127
Joyce, James, 55

Kauffer, E. McKnight, 79–80
Kurz, Barbara, 59

La Fontaine, Jean de, 35–37
LaForgue, Jules, 34
Lantern (Bryn Mawr), 31
Lawrence, D. H., 48, 58–59, 75
Little Review, The, 2, 9

Martz, Louis L., 48
Marvell, Andrew, 54
Metaphysical argumentation, 47–54
Mitchell, Roger, 127
Monroe, Harriet, 2
Moore, John Warner, 10
Moore, Marianne, works:
  "The Accented Syllable," 99
  "Armor's Undermining Modesty," 7,
    19, 79
  "A Bold Virtuoso," 34
  "Brooklyn from Clinton Hill," 13
  "A Burning Desire to Be Explicit," 63
  "The Cantos" [review of Ezra Pound's
    work], 24
  "A Carriage from Sweden," 112
  Collected Poems, 6, 60
  *The Complete Poems of Marianne
    Moore*, 4, 6, 31, 57, 82, 100
  "Critics and Connoisseurs," 1, 36–37,
    43, 47, 49, 50–54, 55, 71, 74, 116
  "Dock Rats," 6, 10, 14, 124
  "Efforts of Affection," 80
  "England," 15, 100, 101
  The Fables of La Fontaine, 5
  "Feeling and Precision," 23, 27, 35,
    43, 99

"Four Quartz Crystal Clocks," 119–
  20
"The Fish," 85
"Granite and Steel," 59
"A Grave" ("The Graveyard"), 15, 17–
  18, 87–88
"Half Deity," 6, 89
"He 'Digesteth Harde Yron,'" 27, 121
"Henry James as a Characteristic
  American," 13, 21, 28, 29. *See also*
  James, Henry
"The Hero," 31, 40, 57–62, 112–13.
  See also "Part of a Novel, Part of a
  Poem, Part of a Play"
"His Shield," 32, 121
"Idiosyncrasy and Technique," 121
"I May, I Might, I Must" ("Progress"),
  1, 45–46, 50, 102
"In Distrust of Merits," 70–75, 95,
  113
"Is Your Town Nineveh," 43
"The Jerboa," 32, 88
"'Keeping Their World Large,'" 70,
  71, 111
"The Labours of Hercules," 72–73
A Marianne Moore Reader, 6, 44, 60
"Marriage," 29–30, 33, 48, 57, 87, 120
"Melancthon" ("Black Earth"), 6, 17,
  33, 43, 54, 87, 108
"Mercifully," 62
"The Mind, Intractable Thing," 31, 96
"The Mind Is an Enchanting Thing,"
  6–7, 43, 77, 87, 88, 92–96, 113–16
"The Monkeys" ("My Apish
  Cousins"), 15, 33–34, 37, 47, 54
"No Swan So Fine," 6, 63–66, 77, 99,
  107, 118
"Novices," 29, 30, 85–86, 87
Observations, 3, 10, 13, 14, 18, 46, 47,
  77, 117
"An Octopus," 56–57, 86–87, 120
O to Be a Dragon, 45, 82
"Old Tiger," 6, 18–25, 32–33, 37, 43,
  47, 49, 54, 56, 88–91, 104, 107
Omaggio a Marianne Moore, 18
"The Pangolin," 41, 89–92, 111
"The Paper Nautilus," 1, 7, 40, 41,
  66–68, 99, 121
"Part of a Novel, Part of a Poem, Part

of a Play," 57–62, 112–13. *See also*
  "The Steeple-Jack," "The Student,"
  and "The Hero"
"The Past Is the Present," 35, 47, 87,
  103
"People's Surroundings," 7, 15, 38, 87,
  118
"Peter," 100, 101–2
"Picking and Choosing," 100, 101
"The Plumet Basilisk," 28, 89
Poems, 2, 14, 16–17, 99, 100, 124
"Poetry," 33, 35, 54, 55, 87, 100
Predilections, 6
"Profit Is a Dead Weight," 27
"Radical," 6, 77–79
"Reinforcements," 70
"Reticent Candor," 6, 28
"Roses Only," 54
Selected Poems, 3, 6, 47
"Silence," 56
"Spenser's Ireland," 80
"The Steeple-Jack," 57–62, 112–13.
  See also "Part of a Novel, Part of a
  Poem, Part of a Play"
"The Student," 14, 29, 57–62, 112–
  13. *See also* "Part of a Novel, Part
  of a Poem, Part of a Play"
"Style," 94
"Sun," 44–45, 47, 55, 82–85, 107,
  111, 126
Tell Me, Tell Me, 63, 82
"That Harp You Play So Well" ("That
  Harp You Played So Well"), 45, 47,
  102–3
"Those Various Scalpels," 30–31, 37–
  38
"To a Chameleon" ("You Are Like
  the Realistic Product of an Idealis-
  tic Search for Gold at the Foot of
  the Rainbow"), 82, 107
"To an Egyptian Pulled Glass Bottle
  in the Shape of a Fish," 57, 107
"To an Intra-Mural Rat," 46
"To Military Progress," 38, 45, 46–47,
  55, 70, 81, 105
"To a Prize Bird" ("To Bernard Shaw:
  A Prize Bird"), 47
"To Statecraft Embalmed," 38, 55,
  104, 105–6, 108, 109

"To a Steam Roller," 49–50, 53, 55,
  108–9
"To William Butler Yeats on Tagore,"
  47
"We Will Walk like the Tapir," 121
"What Are Years," 24–25, 121–22,
  125
What Are Years, 6, 29, 34, 89, 99
"When I Buy Pictures," 18, 33, 100,
  101–2
Marianne Moore Newsletter, 5, 12, 117–
  18, 124
Metropolis, 27, 28–29, 38–39
Moore, Mary Warner, 10, 11
Murphy, Thomas P., 99

Nemerov, Howard (Voice of America
  broadcast, 1963), 14, 17, 31–32, 120–
  21
New York Times Magazine, The, 63, 65,
  119
New Yorker, The, 62

Others, 10, 47

Phaedrus, 35
Phillip, Percy, 63, 111
Poetry, 2, 46, 47, 57, 64
Pound, Ezra, 6, 9–11, 15–18, 21–25, 34,
  46, 55, 75, 81, 110
Process of obtaining knowledge by
  sight, 43, 55

Quarterly Review of Literature, The,
  "Marianne Moore Issue," 4

Ransom, John Crowe, 4
Rimbaud, Arthur, 33
Revisions, 17–25, 60, 82, 99–101
Rhetorical conversations, 45–47
Rosenbach Museum & Library, 5, 28,
  77, 126
Rosenthal, M. L., 126

Saintsbury, George, 64
Self-corrective assertions, 56–57, 109,
  110
Shakespeare, William, 55, 106–7
Shaw, George Bernard, 11

Skelton, John, 44, 46, 111
Song of Songs, The, 31
Spenser, Edmund, 117
Stapleton, Laurence, 4, 98, 117, 124, 127
Steinman, Lisa, 124
Stevens, Wallace, 4, 34, 38, 48, 59, 75
Syllabic verse, 3–4, 101–2

Tipyn O'Bob (Bryn Mawr), 45

Tomlinson, Charles, 98
Tuve, Rosamund, 51, 125

Valéry, Paul, 69, 77, 79, 126
Vaughan, Henry, 52, 54

War, 67–75
Warner, John Riddle, 10, 11
Whitman, Walt, 13–15, 127

A Note on the Author

Grace Schulman is Poetry Editor of *The Nation*, and was Director of the Poetry Center, 92nd Street YM-YWHA, from January 1974 through June 1984. She is the author of two collections of poems, *Burn Down the Icons* and *Hemispheres*, co-translator of Pablo Antonio Cuadra's *Songs of Cifar and the Sweet Sea* and award-winning translator of T. Carmi's *At the Stone of Losses*. Her poems have been widely anthologized, and her poems, essays, and translations have appeared in publications such as the *New Yorker, Hudson Review, American Poetry Review*, and *Poetry*. A former vice-president of the P.E.N. American Center, she is a professor of English at Baruch College, C.U.N.Y., where she won the first President's Award for Creative Excellence. She has taught writing workshops at Princeton, Columbia, Wesleyan, Bennington, and Hofstra.